HIGHWAY TO DESTINY

To The Sisters of the Convent with grateful thanks for the love & care of Rozanne* over the many years

Love

John

HIGHWAY TO DESTINY
– Memories of a Lifetime –

John Butler

JANUS PUBLISHING COMPANY
London, England

First published in Great Britain 2008
by Janus Publishing Company Ltd,
105-107 Gloucester Place,
London W1U 6BY

www.januspublishing.co.uk

Copyright © John Butler 2008
British Library Cataloguing-in-Publication Data
A catalogue record for this book is available from the British Library

ISBN 978-1-85756-688-8

All rights reserved. No part of this publication may be reproduced, stored in a retrieval system or transmitted in any form or by any means, electric, mechanical, photocopying, recording or otherwise, without the prior permission of the publisher.

The right of John Butler to be identified as the author of this work has been asserted by him in accordance with the Copyright, Designs and Patents Act 1988.

Cover Design: Janus Publishing
Photograph supplied by John Butler

Printed and bound in Great Britain

Contents

Introduction	1
Preface	3
Early Memories	5
Our Heritage	21
John Norman and Ethel Gertrude – My Parents	27
The War Years	33
Wartime Home-Guard Incidents	43
Alice	47
Bellington	53
Whytehouse	59
African Voyage	71
Maciene	79
Bryngolau	115
Blaenplwyf	123
Kidderminster Young Farmers' Club Fiftieth Anniversary	127
Selattyn and Retirement	133
Other Thoughts	137
Religious Thoughts on my Life	141

Dedication

To the women in my life: my mother, my wife and my daughters.

> Lord, temper with tranquility
> My manifold activity,
> That I may do my work for Thee
> In very great simplicity.
>
> Sister Lacta Mary C.S.M.V.

Introduction

Having reached a goodly number of years, I am liable to bore family and friends with my stories of actual facts (subject to an ageing memory). Over the course of eighty years, I have had an unusual number of experiences (so I am told), both here and abroad, which others may also be interested to hear of.

My daughter Rozanne suggested that I record some of them and offered to edit and produce a booklet if I did so. Bridget, my younger daughter, offered to type them up on to the computer, not realising that they could run to nearly 50,000 words. Each written word is true to fact, as is each and every name and place, subject, of course, to fallibility of my now ageing memory. I have come from a long line of farming stock and as well as farming, I have drifted into various other occupations, including sailor, builder, missionary and now author. My thanks go out to Rozanne and Bridget for encouraging me, and for doing and compiling all the work necessary to see it through to final publication. I hope you enjoy reliving it with me.

John

Preface

Whilst deciding on the name of my memoirs, my mind has drifted from the days when I was told to keep the pigeons (or quice, as they are commonly called) off the green spring oilseed rape, grown for sheep feed; I fired both barrels of the old twelve-bore shot gun at them from the hip, and fell over backwards on to the floor.

This led on to middle age and the shooting of an African pigeon in Mozambique, only to find, much to my remorse, how beautiful it actually was in its green-feathered form, leaving me unable to eat it as originally intended.

I later found myself staying with an old friend, Mat (ex-farm student at the Whytehouse) at his home in Marandellas; Southern Rhodesia as it was then. The homestead was set in a large hollow, surrounded by mature trees, and one woke to the cooing of pigeons each morning, which made for a lasting memory. The area beyond the trees was noted for its large stones as big as houses, balanced three high and teetering as if on the verge of falling.

Nowadays, I awake to the cooing of breeding doves and pigeons in the trees in my own garden, and I wonder at nature and its glories, and as to how it can all become jumbled up – from that twelve-bore gun to my wartime rifle and today's bird feeder; from those pesky quice and the beautiful green plumage of the shot-meal to the cooing from my cottage trees and the tranquillity of it all. Still, I suppose it's a bit like receiving identical presents on a birthday, a wedding or an anniversary – 'it's the thought that counts'.

As a child in the 1930s, at the tender age of 9 or 10 years old, I rode the shire horses for 5 miles to the blacksmiths to be shod at Drayton Forge, where I was intrigued on one such occasion to watch them put a strengthening band of iron around the rim of a wooden wheel. The hubs, I believe, were made of holly, the spokes of ash and the circumference of oak. The huge iron tyre was cut and angled to size, and then heated in the furnace to high temperatures. The wheel was then laid in a great stone or concrete mould of convex shape for the hub, and the tyre was then hammered home with much sizzling over the wooden core. When in place, having burnt its way to some degree, it would be quenched with buckets of water to cool it and to shrink it tight. Once cooled, the wheel was spun on an axle and tuned up with tiny wedges hammered into the hub to get a true balance.

No wonder the pioneers could rely on the wagons to cross America and through the rough hinterlands of Africa. Unfortunately, Harry Skinner, his father and his uncle have now all passed away and the smithy no longer makes anything like it any more, and it is with this in mind that I am reminded of the following rendition:

>The Blacksmith hanging up his tools,
>
>My sledge and hammer declin'd,
>
>My bellows too have lost their wind,
>
>My fires extinct, my forge archaic,
>
>And in the dust my vice is laid,
>
>My coal is spent, my irons gone
>
>My nails are drove, my work is done.
>
>   ANON

Early Memories

My earliest memory is of being in hospital having my tonsils out at the age of four, and I can still see that ward today, and that was back in 1927. The nursing home was opposite the then cattle market at Hagley, where Chappel and Foster held their weekly sales. The market was interesting in that it was for fat stock, which was probably consumed in Birmingham some ten miles further on. Mr Arthur Chappel used to drive his dog cart the eight miles to Bromsgrove every evening after the sale, whether in daylight or in darkness, with the whole day's takings about his person and was never mugged!

At the Churchill Church of England village primary school, a door slammed shut in the cloakroom on a windy day, and I had put my hand out to stop it, just as our cricketers might take a catch, with the result being that my finger was taken with it. Wedged in between the lock and the door frame, it was flattened out, just like a twopence coin. Wrapping a rag around the wound, I ran the one mile home in eighteen inches of snow, and after a memorable journey, with the tyres wrapped in chains, I was sent to see Dr Meldon in Stourbridge. It was folded back and left to heal, and that finger is still half inside out to this day. Another time, I was foolishly teasing a school friend, who tethered the family goat on his way to school and collected it on his way home at night. I suppose it was deserved, but he swiped me with the three-foot tethering peg and it cut my cheekbone wide open, resulting in another trip to Dr Meldon to be stapled up with metal clips.

My father and uncle were in partnership working a large farm in those days, and one of their ventures was silage making. A horse-drawn mower was used to mow oats, tic beans, peas and vetch mixture, and this was hand loaded on to carts and hauled to a wide clamp. A trace horse was then attached to the cart to climb the steep stack, which also helped consolidate the crop. One day, the driver of the mower was distracted, and the two horses galloped off with the whirring mower in tow. They made it through the gateway and turned down the road for home by Cut Throat Lane, taking up the entire width of the lane. A shepherd was driving his flock of sheep in their path and somehow, they diverted the horses around a nearby tree. The shepherd was heard to remark with relief, "That would have pared their bloody foot rot sharpish if they buggers hadna stopped short", and the wagoner's response was, "Dint they buggers go, ahh!"

The sheep that farmers kept in those days were Shropshires or Clun Forests, and at dipping time, the ewes had to be lifted clean off the floor and gently lowered into the dip, tail first and on their backs. The local bobby would be notified and it would be his job to ensure that each sheep was immersed for at least one and a half minutes, culminating in a dunking on her way out to the draining pens. This set-up was very laboured. The Modern process, in which the sheep were left to run along a corridor, where, at a given point, the floor would tip up and in they went, untouched by the human hand, evolved. Dipping left the fleece clean and impregnated with a detergent mix, which killed the maggot fly and saved them from being eaten alive by masses of maggots, which would be supplemented by yet more eggs by the hour.

Mutton, mature sheep meat, was from the larger breeds of sheep – Shropshires, Clun Forests and Oxfords in particular – which grew into huge sheep, albeit they were slow maturers. These were fattened later in the year on root crops, and made large joints of meat for the families with large appetites, and they were also so much tastier than the smaller breeds. Later, when it became fashionable to eat smaller meals and families had less staff and family members to cater for, the smaller joint and younger lamb took precedent on the dining table, and this came from the Hampshire; ewes mostly, crossed with Suffolk rams. Other small breeds, such as Southdowns, can be used, too. The hill sheep we see today are a very hardy animal, and can live at higher altitudes on poorer herbage, but the lambs make for sweet and tender meat. It is only in their second year that the young ewes are hardy enough to remain high up in the hills throughout the winter months, and they spend their first winter on lowland levels. Dorset Horn sheep are particularly fertile and produce as many as three crops of lambs in two years.

Friesian cattle were imported from the Dutch in about 1931, and they influenced the downfall of the traditional shorthorns. They had large bodies for the benefit of the meat trade and gave higher yields of milk, even if not so rich. This was followed by importations of the Holsteins from Canada, which had large, bony bodies, but looked like the Friesian, and which outstripped them all in milk production. This then led to a decline in the Ayrshire breed, too. The Jerseys were kept going for their quality of cream, easy calving and smaller size, meaning more cows per acre or per ton of feed.

Quice is a Worcestershire name for wood pigeons, which used to wreak havoc on the green rape and cabbage grown for the sheep in winter. They used to fly over in their droves and as long as you remained still in your hide, they would circle and land above you, so that increasing numbers of shots could be fired in order to thin their numbers and to help fill the old stewing pots in the process.

Farmers always kept a twelve-bore shotgun on the premises to keep down vermin and to provide food for the household. Foxes, rabbits, rats, quice, crows, magpies and ravens were considered pests, but pheasant, partridge, hare and wild duck were delicacies to be had. The gun also served to keep pigeons away from the green rape, kale or other crops, and also, if he so desired, it could provide a good day's sport shooting with friends. During the 1930s, when the Estate Shoot was being held, I was told that whilst the men were off with their guns, Lady Cobham, the estate owner's wife, was known to have spent the day sitting darning socks until they returned.

A yearling sheep was butchered at home and labelled as mutton, as was a young ewe which ailed, and it was much tastier than the immature lamb we get today. The Easter lamb market was just as important as the Christmas Fair, with young potatoes and peas made much of, but not always possible. Eggs and kidney beans were preserved for the winter months. The eggs were immersed in water glass, a liquid which sealed the shells, and the beans were sliced and salted in layers in salt-glazed jars. Collecting the eggs from free-range hens was often a hazardous occupation, as hens laid away, and you could not tell just by looking at them as to how old they were. By placing them in water and by leaving out the 'floaters', we survived to see another day. Geese were considered to be a pest round the corn stacks, as they quickly learnt to pull the corn out by the stalk, with the ears of corn following, but the ducks would lay in wait and grab the emerging feast, leaving the goose to try its luck again. In no time at all, they could undermine the stacks by as much as two or three feet, leaving wastage, an angry farmer and a mess in their wake.

Swearing was not necessarily used as a bad word in those days, but rather to emphasise a point, and it became a general and accepted part of rural vocabulary. Some men became so adept at using every third word thus, that they could talk amongst themselves for a quarter of an hour before repeating themselves and every one knew what the other was trying to say with clarity.

My early working days at home were adventurous, but very heavy manually. Seed wheat was delivered in two-and-a-quarter cwt sacks, and fertilisers came in two cwt sacks. Manure was all handled manually, having been dug out from the pens, loaded on to horse carts and dumped into five or six heaps about 4 yards apart on the land. This would then be spread in the fields at a rate of 20 tons per acre, all done by hand, using hand forks. Years ago, the ploughing was done using horses pulling single-furrow ploughs, which used to turn over about an acre a day. This took two or three horses, and the ploughman walked behind, covering 12 miles per day. These days, a man sits in a heated cab driving a 130 hp tractor, pulling a multi-furrowed plough, turning up to 20 or 30 acres per day.

The seed potatoes were also planted by hand, having been dropped into the ridges at distances of approximately 18 inches. Sugar beet was sown into furrows with the corn drill and then singled out by hand. It was then cultivated with a single horse hoe, before latterly being pulled, topped and hauled by hand. We took great pride in our work; ploughing, for instance, with a team of horses, covering, on average, an acre per day, 12 miles, in all weathers, except for snow. Woe betide anyone who walked on our furrows before the field was finished, at which point the farmer would happily harrow it down for the next crop. Drilling seeds, ploughing, ridging and so on was an art in itself, as the horses would have to be driven accurately in straight lines across the fields, making the task of hoeing much easier. In those days, the implements would take two pairs of hands to control them and with only one pair for both jobs this took real skill and ability. This task is still performed today, of course, only it is 'horsepower' instead that is used nowadays to drive the machinery.

Ponies and floats were often the only means of transportation in those days; it being a light utility two-wheeled, one-horse vehicle used for all purposes. It took the farmer to market and delivered livestock and light loads, in addition to performing the milk round twice daily.

All milking was performed by hand, with six or eight cows per person, and the milkers sat on three-legged stools (non-wobblers), with an open bucket supported between their legs. This would then be emptied into larger, open buckets, which, when full, would then be carried to the dairy adjoining the farmhouse, where it would be poured through a filter into a 16-gallon churn. These churns would then be lifted on to the float, along with a 4-gallon lidded bucket and two measures for delivery to each village in turn.

The milkman would walk up the garden paths and pour the set quantity of milk from his bucket into the waiting jug, before covering it with its crocheted cloth. The horse was so accustomed to the work at hand that it would walk up the road on its own and wait at the next gate, whilst the milkman (otherwise known as a roundsman) took short cuts across the gardens with his load. The milk was delivered warm, straight from the cow in those days, and I have even seen a cow's foot plonked into her milker's bucket before now; and on the odd occasion, it has been known to be a bit on the green side from the cow having eaten too much ivy.

Ours was a pedigree shorthorn herd, with bloodlines called Wild Eyes, Countess and so on, and the bull was registered as a premium stock bull, which carried a subsidy and was available for use in all the local small farms in order to improve the quality of the herds nationally. All such services were recorded in a book, which was inspected and signed by the local policeman every month.

Meals in the 1930s and earlier had the provision of food for labour-intensive farm workers in mind. Many young men lived in and so the farmhouses were large enough to accommodate them, often with a hired maid to help with the running of the house. Sunday was deemed to be a 'Joint Day' – perhaps with roast beef and Yorkshire pudding served to all. Monday might be poultry – perhaps a sickly, old, or otherwise hen. On a Tuesday, a rabbit or a hare might be stewed with plenty of potatoes. Wednesday, would perhaps be mutton, with no questions asked, initially served steaming hot and afterwards, cold or in field sandwiches. Thursday might be a hotpot made from everything that had been left over from the week's meals, with lots of onions and potatoes. Fridays were similar or would consist of whatever happened to turn up, like pheasant, partridge or wood pigeon (quice). Each meal was always followed by a pudding of some sort or another, with suet being a favourite, or plum, damson or apple tart, with a helping of custard. Tea on Fridays often had a little bromide added on the quiet, to quell his antics over the weekend. This was not needed so much during the weekdays, as the long hours and heavy work had the same effect.

Breakfasts never altered: porridge, belly bacon (three-inch wide slices of boiled white bacon fat), sausage, eggs and toast to mop up the liquid fat. This was burnt up during the morning and tea then only needed to be bread, butter and jam, and maybe a cake, with a hot cup of tea or cocoa to go to bed on.

Farmers didn't usually make good gardeners, as they could produce so much more in a field (with horses and implements), than they could by hand in the same amount of time. The wagoners, cowmen, shepherds and staff with the tied cottages were the gardeners, and with the help of manure from the pigsties, they could be guaranteed to produce a good vegetable patch, and it was thus that recycling started all those years ago. Household waste was fed to the pig, the pig fertilised the garden, and the garden waste was also fed back to the pig. The pig then became the staple food of the household to be served with the garden veg, which, in turn, was dug back into the ground in the form of sewage waste from the earth closet up the garden path; recycling existed even then! This way of living left little waste for burning and no tins were involved at all.

During our early years, our school was located about a mile away, but during our later years, we had to walk two miles just to catch the bus to town and arrived back through a small wooded area under the darkness of night, which was not particularly pleasant.

Our first radio was on a turntable, called a Lion. It required two batteries; one large dry battery and one wet accumulator, which had to be charged every week. By 1938, I recall a shopkeeper, a certain Mr John Russell, Coventry Street, Kidderminster and his Austin 16 saloon, used to drive out five miles distant with the charged batteries, where he would wire them in and charge a fee of 6d (about 3 pence).

It was not until 1936 that we first had electricity, in the form of a motorised generator, with two long leads and eight bulbs about the size of small jugs. This contraption was installed in the utility room (back kitchen), and fed the house in two directions, nailed to the beams with barbed-wire staples. When a bulb failed on installation, the man carried a spare one with him and I recall someone having once said, "Now turn it on ... slowly." Whilst it was noisy, it was also so much better than the paraffin lamps, with their smelly, smoking wicks and yellow light, which had to be refilled every day.

Valor Perfection paraffin heaters were often used for cooking and the flame used to creep up producing oily smog, and many a time after a thorough cleaning through, one was met by a black stinking fog from the kitchen, and the oily smog would permeate the room.

Every house in those days reared a pig, which was fed on the household scraps; their diet was also boosted by boiling some of the smallest of potatoes and some greens. When the pig reached about 16 score (320 lb) in weight and during the early part of the winter, the 'travelling pig killer' was called, when the pig would be led from the sty by a halter or a leg rope and taken squealing to the bench; once pushed sideways on to the bench and the knife had done its deadly deed, the pig lay silent and the squealing stopped. The corpse was then laid on a bed of straw, which was set fire to, to remove the hair and bristles, and then hot water (three parts boiling to one cold) was used to scrub the entire carcass vigorously. This not only cleaned them, but it also turned even black pigs into white ones. The stomach was then opened and the innards were carefully removed – some of the intestines were retained for sausage skins, and some was reserved for chitterlings – and with the exception of the stomach and squeal, everything else was viewed as food to be consumed.

The liver, brains, heart, kidneys and other offal were made into faggots for frying, and the head, trotters, ears and tail was reserved for brawn. The carcass was then hung for twenty-four hours or so before cutting up, to allow the meat to drain and set. Once cut down, the meat was placed on to a cold slab where the flitches (sides of bacon) were salted. This salt was used to cure the bacon, with some saltpetre being used for the thick shoulder and ham bone parts, and brown sugar was then rubbed in together with the salt. The bacon was then packed meat-side down for a week, before being turned face upwards for three weeks. It would then be hung from meat hooks from the kitchen ceiling, where it would remain until consumed.

There was no such thing as eating out, as there was no spare cash to do so, and because of the fact that except for the odd 'do's, there was nowhere to go anyway. Cider and perry were produced from the orchard and were matured with raisins in 60-gallon barrels. Some called it Scrumpy, others vinegar, but when young, it was thirst quenching and potent, and proved to be particularly good in the hayfields throughout the hot summer's days or when threshing in thick dust in the midst of winter.

Haymaking was not an easy task in itself. My father said that the 'seeds' of hay must be hand-turned in order to protect the leaf and seeds, and so large wooden hand rakes were used to turn the swathes. These swathes would be carefully cocked with hay forks, using a folding method, and the folds would then be placed one above the other, as wafers, so as to mature in watertight conditions, until being pitched on to the wagons and stored in the barns. If cut young and matured thus, the quality of the product was excellent, but if cut when older, with more weight per acre, and turned with a machine and gathered quickly, it could mean that it was no better than straw. Knots in the stems also posed a problem, and, if not cured enough, the hay would be susceptible to mould or may even catch fire due to a build up of heat, thus being rendered useless.

Mangolds and swedes, like beetroot, were inclined to bleed, and so the tops would be twisted off, rather than being cut, even the roots, to be used as stockfeed. These were then put through a hand-turned pulper, which proved to be hard work on the handler each day.

The process of shearing was updated with time from hand clippers to machine clippers, but the poor chap turning the handle tired easily. The fleeces were rolled and tied with a twisted cord of wool from the neck of the fleece, and placed into huge wool sacks. Before any shearing began, many sheep were washed in the brook to remove the oily lanolin from them, and all had to be 'dagged' to remove locks of wool matted with muck from the hindquarters, being careful not to get them mixed up with the straw, otherwise the price would suffer. Foot rot was a never-ending chore and a great nuisance, and each animal would have to be upturned to be foot trimmed, and any infected hoofs were treated with a lard and vitriol compound.

The rams would then have to be removed and isolated in the autumn, only to be introduced to the flock again at the appropriate time for the farm's system. Lowland farms wanted Christmas/New Year lambs for the Easter market; upland farms wanted spring lambs, when the grass was growing again, and these lambs became stores for fattening on turnips in the winter.

Cockerels were fattened, as were the turkeys and geese, for Christmas sales. Indian gamecocks were also sometimes used, but they were very aggressive towards the young cocks, and bloody battles ensued. The game birds had long inside spurs and fought by leaping over their rivals and kicking backwards, thereby cutting the opponent's head to ribbons.

At Christmas time, the geese were put into the sheep pens on straw at market, with their legs and wings tied together. Each had a note tied to it, denoting its weight, which was duly announced at the point of sale. These pens held about six geese in each and the bidding was done on the first goose, which the purchaser was then given the option of having, along with as many more in the pen as they cared for at the same price.

On one particular Christmas, in about 1937/1938, I recall the landlord Ralph Barker of the Anchor pub at Cauncil having desired a goose for his wife. He dealt quite a lot in pigs and on this particular day, a very raw and cold one, he had drunk rather too much ale at the Hagley pub before the sale with his cronies, and all he could remember was 'goose for my wife'. Anyway, the sale commenced and he duly bought the first goose, at which point the auctioneer asked him how many he wanted. His reply was, "Ooh, I'll take the lot", which meant all six. The same thing happened with the next pens, too, and he eventually arrived home that night with sixty live geese just six days before Christmas. I believe his wife was not amused, and she had to organise pluckers to come in from the village of Cookley to dress them all, in time for the Kidderminster dressed-poultry sale just three days later.

Turkeys running loose with the hens seemed to get blackhead, which killed them off a month or so before reaching maturity. The most successful rearers either kept no hens, or put them in pens two foot off the ground on netting. Geese didn't seem to be susceptible to many problems, but were a curse to pluck; first you plucked them, and then started over again, in order to remove the layer of fine down against the skin – as was the case with ducks, too.

Poultry houses were placed on the stubbled fields, so that the hens could feed on the shed corn cheaply for a week or two, but these houses had to be secured safely at night, so that the fox could not get at them. Even so, he was wily enough to win sometimes; when a fox kills poultry, it does not kill to eat; it kills for fiendishness and kills the lot, taking only the last one for food, rarely returning for another corpse. Carrion crows are also a pest to livestock and when a ewe is cast (lying upside down) or lying down giving birth, they peck out their eyes.

Horses were generally hardy, but needed expert care and affection, and the stables had cobbled floors so as to get air to their hooves to avoid lameness. If a young mare was ever to be bred, it was considered to be a good idea to let her foal at three years of age, before she began her working life, and it would then be fine to breed from her again ten years later, with a comparatively lower foaling risk. The kickers were a nuisance though, and beware of the one with a wall eye (eye squinting outwards)! White hooves were softer than dark ones and were inclined to split; however, the really intelligent horses were like sheep dogs and a pleasure to work with. One horse could plough all day or hoe the crops merely by the farmer talking to them, and they would obey the command automatically – come back left, gee off, right, gee up, go, whoa there, stop, git on, hurry up, steady now and so on – without the farmer even having to use the reins. The collars had to be serviced in order to prevent the animals from getting sore shoulders and these were placed over the head upside down, only being turned over when having passed the ears, so as to get the eyes through the contraption at the widest point.

Young horses were broken to work by being harnessed between two trained horses, leaving them with no other option than to follow, and thus, they gradually became more confident and more accustomed to receiving verbal commands. However, if fear prevailed, they would shy, take off, or worse still.

The sheepdogs were more than worth their weight in gold; they were your pal, your guard, your legs and your closest friend. You would worship each other, but one was considered lucky to get more than one or two like that in one's lifetime. They were one-man dogs and could be ruined if they had more than one person using them. You could put them in a field of mixed stock, and they would be able to separate them and then bring you back any breed you so desired, be it poultry, sheep, pigs or cattle, and this would all be done without so much as disturbing the others. If you needed to move a flock elsewhere, it was possible for the farmer to walk in front in the knowledge that every single sheep was still following behind, safely shepherded and without any aggro.

Sheep worrying was also a problem, and not only would the errant dog chase the sheep to the point of exhaustion, but it could also pull the insides of a live sheep out, cause the sheep to abort or subject it to the pain of giving birth to twisted lambs at lambing time.

Sheep worrying is an awful sight to behold and I vividly recall one occasion when an Irish wolfhound and another sheepdog set about our ewes, which had been penned in to feed on turnips behind wire netting and were therefore unable to escape. Some had their skulls crushed in; others had their sides ripped open, displaying their innards. Those which were only bitten aborted or went septic. We managed to trace the owners of the dogs, who insisted that the dogs belonged to their young daughter and we could either accept a small offering from them or sue the daughter for all she had. The same dogs also worried a neighbouring flock before eventually being caught, having killed fifteen fattening sheep in a field next to ours.

As if these trials and tribulations were not bad enough, the farmer also had to contend with health problems, such as lung worms, orf, bloat, foot rot, blackhead, mastitis, TB, foot and mouth, erysipelas and swine fever in their stock.

Farmers' sons were deemed to be free labour, and would be expected to help, with the intention of starting off on their own or taking over in later years. My pay was £6 per year if I was lucky, including food, board and clothing until reaching 20 years of age.

Market days not only kept the farmer abreast of the prices, but also of fashion, trade and the outlook for the future. It was quite a social occasion, and it also meant that the farmer could stay in touch with the trade reps for updates and have a drink amongst friends. A farmer was in constant competition with his contemporaries, because a good deal for one was a poor deal for the other. Healthy competition was good, but it required certain amounts of diplomacy sometimes in order to both get your own way and to remain friends after the resultant action.

Shows were viewed as being a special day out, or a day off, after the stock had been seen to earlier in the day. At such events, the reps were able to offer hospitality in return for all the farmhouse cups of tea they could possibly consume; the best of everything was sure to be on display and you could compare notes with the judge's decisions and generally enjoy the occasion as a community.

My first experience of being conned was when I was offered a shilling (5p) if I could prove that I could milk my first cow, which was a small fortune in those days. Being on the small side, the breed being the larger pedigree shorthorn Wild Eyes and Countesses, the teats seemed a long way up for me to reach, but I managed it and in the course of events, got my just reward. Imagine my indignation, therefore, on being rewarded with the directive to milk two of them before going to school for free each day thereafter!

As a lad of about 8 or 9 years, I looked up to our ageing shepherd Amos Roberts. He would hold my hand as we surveyed the sheep, and he had a very keen eye that could spot a ewe in trouble at twenty paces. He was ancient to me in those days, and I looked on him in awe, as he told me how he helped to build the railway viaduct at Blakedown all those years before, his own son being a ganger throughout his life on the railways.

My second experience of being conned was as a stockman in charge, where I was given a chit to sign accepting a £25 gratuity from the sellers exporting livestock, but later on when I checked I discovered much to my chagrin that the centre notes had been folded – the clerk had taken £5 for himself.

At about eight years old in around 1932 we were taken in the farm van to visit the Hammersleys at Edgebold Farm in Lichfield. As it was a Sunday, we all wore our Sunday best, sporting highly polished shoes, as was the custom on special occasions. "Now before you go out for the day, go round to the toilet, there's good children." Churchill farm toilets were a respectfully built edifice, covering a chamber known as an earth-closet, as opposed to a flush toilet which we use today. With no water, fire ash was used to absorb the liquid and smell, and it was basically a small room with a bench in which were three different sized holes with hinged covers.

During our last brief visit, a muted bleat was heard from far below; someone had not put the lid down and a cade lamb (orphan) had jumped up and disappeared down the hole. The memory of seeing my father at full stretch to his shoulders trying to grab hold of the lamb is still with me today. Needless to say, he eventually managed to drag it to safety by its ear, where he proceeded to wipe it on the grass, before placing it, smelling ripe and fruitful, in the straw of the barn.

This outing had been particularly interesting for me, where our friends had put two cade lambs, a piglet and a puppy all in the same old-fashioned pigsty. These creatures all shared the same milk from the same trough and slept together for warmth afterwards in the inner sanctum of a straw bed with the family cat. Anyway, we'd all had a nice day out and had returned in the evening to find total uproar; the lamb had apparently recovered during the day and had gone on a rampage about the village, where he had received short shrift from the neighbours, who were then seen to be waiting on the doorstep to complain about the matter.

Early Memories

Another notable character was George Creed, the estate gamekeeper, who always seemed to wear brown plus fours and used to carry a gun. When poachers started to catch rabbits on his patch using long nets strung across the fields, he used to cut the hawthorn bushes down and drop them at random, thereby foiling the intruders. Then he would wrap the nets up and release the rabbits, without anyone being any the wiser.

As for us, fifty years later, our land was surrounded by plantations harbouring rabbits that used to come out at night and eat and spoil the pastures, so the only solution we found was to lamp them. This entailed driving a tractor, with headlights on full-beam, around the boundaries and shooting the dazzled pests in the process. After one such evening, we were visited by some sporty miners from the valleys in South Wales, who wanted some trophies to take back and impress their contemporaries. We sold about eighty to them at a shilling each, and they were as overjoyed over the transaction as us, hoping to impress their colleagues with their prowess to boot.

In the 1930s at Churchill Farm, all of our corn threshing was done by a travelling contracted 'threshing gang' of Cliff Oakley's. An old tractor, probably an Overtime, was used to thresh the entire corn croppage within a wide radius of Cookley near Kidderminster. His son Cuth followed him in his footsteps with the same tackle. As an aside, Cuth's cousin Robin is known for being the television parliamentary reporter until just recently.

As a young fellow, my literary favourite was Adrian Bell, who wrote *Corduroy*, *The Cherry Tree* and *Silver Lay*. His son Martin Bell is now a well-known war reporter and MP in a white suit. Adrian also compiled the Times crossword for forty-six years, as well as writing a literary piece about his learning exploits as he experienced them, which were parallel with those of my own.

Another of my favourites was A. G. Street, who wrote for the *Farmers Weekly* and published several books on farming during the Great Depression. Henderson, being another, wrote *The Farming Ladder* and was a hard-headed businessman, who took apprentices on his Cotswold farm, worked them for about six years for fourteen hours a day and if they could stand the pace, he would then finance them on their own farms.

My father was a great supporter of the NFU and often attended meetings at Worcester and it was during one of those meetings one Saturday that I was told (never asked) to take the cattle off the clover field at 2.00 p.m. By the time I got there, many of them were suffering from bloat, where gases from the rich clover distended the stomach and pressed on the diaphragm, resulting in death for the poor animal. At about 14 or 15 years of age, I dashed home in a panic to fetch a carving knife, and then walked them all, to ease the pain, but when two staggered, I knew it was near the end and used the knife like a trocar, and went in just in front of the hip and punctured the stomach. This nightmare continued until they were safe to leave on their own, and, fortunately, only one died in the end. A cattle lorry was called and we dragged the bled corpse up the ramp in a succession of one, two three, heaves, arriving at the slaughter house in time to save the carcass for human consumption. Even though father was not amused at the time, I thought I had done pretty well considering how many deaths had been averted.

At Churchill in the 1930s, coal was delivered to Blakedown Station at £1 10s 0d a ton and an 8-ton wagonload was purchased every autumn to enable us to get through the winter. It was delivered in enormous lumps of 55 lb or more, and Mother was expected to use a hammer to break it up on each visit. Carts would be sent out to fetch it back along the 2-mile journey from Blakedown train depot, with a load carrying a mere 1 ton per horse and cart load. The horses were not accustomed to traffic, especially that of railway engines, and everyone was glad when the job was over. Our Mr Rutter, who ran the grocery store at Blakedown, from where we got our gobstoppers at four a penny, was a white-bearded old soul, who used to walk to Kidderminster from Blakedown every Tuesday, which was some three-and-a-half miles away. He used to pull a sack truck behind him, on which he used to stack his new supplies before dragging them back home to his shop in the afternoon.

On the way to the sweet shop, we used to pass the coalman, Mr Wilson, who had recently changed his horse for a younger model, only this one was scared of trains. Each day, Mr Wilson used to go out for more coal from the yard at the station, and the horse used to refuse to cross the track to deliver their load on the way back. "I'll make you face it," yelled the exasperated driver, who promptly reversed the horse and cart over to the other side for some time to come, before the horse would go across the line forwards.

Later on, it became my job to walk to Hagley Mart every week with fattened sheep or cattle, in the vain hope of getting a lift home. There were some days when the sheep used to pant from the heat and were difficult to walk, and other days, particularly when having been sheared, when they were like driving a flock of hares. One bullock, the slowest to fatten, was driven on his own and he ran amok through people's gardens, traipsing through cold frames and hedges, eventually knocking down a stack of bicycles, getting his feet entangled in the spokes in the process, before eventually being penned. As the hammer fell on his sale, we scarpered; that is, both myself and my dog Spot.

At about nine years of age, my father informed me that he was expecting a load of store cattle for winter fattening. They were coming by train to Kidderminster that afternoon and I was expected to help the drover to walk them the 5 miles home to Churchill. My father took us to the station and set us on our way, before returning to settle up for the freight and to collect the van. "Don't hurry them – I won't be many minutes behind," he'd said, at which point he left us. By then it was nearly dark, so, without any means of warning traffic from either direction of our approach, we set off at quite a lick. It wasn't long before a bus nearly took us out and words were exchanged between us, not to mention the cars that came squealing to a halt when they'd seen us at the last minute, and it was all rather frightening for all concerned. By the time we reached the railway bridge outside Blakedown, the inevitable happened. A car met us and went slap bang into the herd. His headlamps went flying down the cutting on to the line, his bumper went elsewhere and the driver came at us fully enraged. It went something like this: "Cattle on the highway without lights at night," ... and something about him seeing us all in court for costs and liability. At that very moment, my father appeared – a very forbidding figure in such circumstances. He pointed out that he had been behind the cattle with his lights on at the time of the accident, failing to mention that he was about a mile behind at the time, adding that idiots who drove at such speed with poor lighting wanted locking up, and did he want to take the matter any further? We left the poor motorist, who was now grovelling, and safely escorted the herd home as fast as we possibly could. Needless to say, we never heard any more of the incident.

The year 1932/1933 or thereabouts saw a hard and frosty winter and on the way home from school once, we diverted by the pool dam, which fed the Churchill forge waterwheel, which is now a museum. The pool was iced over to a depth of about three quarters of an inch and one of our gang dared us to go for a skate. As no one volunteered to join him, we were called cowards, so, not wanting to appear cowardly, on I went with him. It was amazing the way the ice dished for some distance around, but as it held, we ventured further out and all may have been well, had we not joined up to give each other a tow. Crash! In we went. Neither of us could swim and we both had our winter coats on, dragging us down. Panic took over, but, by spreading our weight across the unbroken edges, we managed to clamber out, now soaking wet and very, very cold. The instigator said he had been warned not to go near the ice and would get into trouble if found out, so we hatched a cock-and-bull yarn about some delivery boy or other on a bike, who had pushed us in. This would have worked, had our teacher not witnessed it from her window and enquired of our parents as to our health after a couple of days of thawing out in bed. From a near police search and plenty of sympathy, we received a belting for our lies. Such is life when living on bonus points, but at least we are still here to recount the experiences.

Our Heritage

A few years back, I began to write our family tree, but drew a blank after a fire in Cartmel Priory had destroyed some papers, prominent to my search. The furthest back that I could reach was a certain Peter Butler, who died at Myerside and was believed to have been born in about 1650, possibly in Ireland.

My great grandfathers had farmed both ours and several other Cumbrian farms in the district, including Winder Hall and Outerthwaite, which were farms on a large estate probably owned by the Duke of Devonshire's Holker Hall Estate in Furness, Cumbria.

As five unrelated Butler families appeared in the area at the same time from an unknown source, and as it coincided with the arrival of the daughter of the first Duke of Osery, with Mary Butler marrying the first Duke of Devonshire, who owned Holker Hall, it could be that Mary brought with her some Butler family members from the Kilkenny Estates on her marriage, and installed them in Cartmel Parish. The five families were all tradesmen: blacksmith, carrier, hatter (shopkeeper), fishermen and farmers (including ourselves) and are fairly easy to trace down through the decades.

My grandfather was only 12 years old when his own father had died, and the widow could not continue with the tenancy on his death. It was at this point that he was sent to a boarding school in Brampton. From here, at the age of 18, he travelled to Worcestershire with several of his contemporaries, where they started their own careers on various farms around Kidderminster.

His first farm was 'the Castle', owned by the Nott family at Rock, and after a couple of years, they decided that they wanted it vacated for a member of the family who was getting married. His next farm was a hop farm called Claywood near Tenbury, where he suffered a serious setback when he made a loss in the hop trade for two seasons running. It was said if he could have survived the third season, he would have been made; however, he upped and moved to Churchill Farm on the Cobham Estate in the year 1890, and the farm still remains in our family name today, albeit transformed somewhat.

My father John Norman Butler followed his father on his death in 1921 and formed a partnership with his brother Guy. This partnership of Butler Brothers was formed from 1921 through to 1934, at which point my father took over the tenancy of Yieldingtree Farm in Broome, which my brother still farms today, though as owner.

It was at Churchill Farm that my father was born in 1892, as were his children: Betty 1921, myself – John Robert – in 1923, Winnie (Wyn) in 1927 and Peter in 1930 were born. It was a near enough a four hundred acre farm and included the golf links of the Churchill and Blakedown Golf Club.

I am told that my father, as a baby, was stuffed into rabbit burrows, whilst his carer and her beau Will Darby made love on the links – but perhaps that was just old Will bragging. It was his son that I kept company with during the war on defence duty.

My great grandmother was a Rawlinson from Cartmel, and they still live in the district, so I am told, but my grandfather had her maiden name incorporated in his, and so he became John Rawlinson Butler, which seems to have been a usual occurrence during those days.

One of the Butler fishermen still works as a guide over the Kent Sands, near to where the cockle pickers from China drowned in 2004, with a loss of sixteen lives, when the tide cut them off during the night. Apparently, the tide comes in on those flat sands faster than a horse can gallop, and the unwary would have no chance of survival if they were say a mile out working the cockle beds at the turn of the tide.

I met the last remaining member of the blacksmith Butlers in Flookborough Churchyard. She lived with her two brothers, all unmarried, in about 1990. She had been attending her family grave at the time and we kept in touch for a while until what must have been her demise. Alice, my wife, was unimpressed by one particular gravestone there which read: 'In memory of John and Alice Butler 19_ _'.

The Irish contingent, James Butler, kept Bonny Prince Charlie company on the continent for his eight to ten years of exile, and was awarded Kilkenny Castle, Ireland, with twenty per cent of the wine trade tax for his loyalty.

I never met my grandfather – he died before I was born – but by talking to others who did, I believe that he was of sterling worth. During WWI, he was elected by the government to supervise or evict those farmers who could do better; in fact, he even had to dispossess his best friend on those very grounds. He used to break in and show shires at the shows and was never early in the ring. When the judges were nearly ready, the stewards could be heard calling Mr Butler to the ring, at which point, with all eyes on his horse, he would make his grand entry and would often take the prize.

He was over 6 feet tall and was always preceded by his dog and carrying a 6-foot forked walking stick. One day, in Kidderminster Market, someone told him of a bull that had been tied to the tree by the station, which was doing its best to do a Sampson on it. "That will be my bull come in by train today," he said, and loped off to the station. He was said to have brought some cows in round the offender, before cutting him loose. But, by this time, the bull, less than amused, barged straight through the cows and set off down the line towards Hartlebury, where he was eventually overtaken and retrieved, albeit with some fun and games to be had beforehand. Another time, a dealer who had agreed a price for a load of potatoes then tried to haggle over the cost. When it was pointed out that he had been loaded for an agreed price, and when this was not adhered to, my grandfather pulled out his knife and cut the harness, tipping all its contents on to the floor, before instructing the dealer not to come back. After all, a deal was a deal!

I was always led to believe that my grandfather had died from straining to shut the big sliding barn doors, thereby putting his back out. He had reached the house using two brooms as crutches, but had then caught pneumonia and died in bed at 57 years of age. However, his cousin, at the ripe old age of 102, told me that it was, "Nothing of the sort. I came down from Carlisle to nurse him with a brain tumour till he died". You see, such things were never admitted to in those days.

The old Fordson tractors were exposed to the elements behind the driver's seat and one winter, I wore my grandfather's black suit with long tails to keep me warm. I can't imagine why it caused such merriment to see someone ploughing in tails – it was a most practical garment for the job and, if anything, should have appeared to be stately, even if not accompanied by a top hat.

Another story that was told was of my grandfather having once been sold a horse by a gypsy. Word had it that he asked the man in question to mount it and ride it round the field for inspection, but the man had declined, explaining that he had a boil on his bottom. My grandfather mounted it himself and set off across the field, only to be bucked off after a few yards. Being a man of guts and grim determination, he bought the animal (despite pain to both body and pride), 'so as to learn to ride again'.

In the village of Rock (a cherry tree area), it was not unknown for farmers to return from a day of selling cherries in Birmingham Market, with an excess of unsold fruit. These, they would tip into the River Severn over the bridge in Bewdley in a glut year. These cherry orchards have now all gone – obviously a forty mile cart trek was not on.

At Churchill, we had one stockyard devoted to pigs. Rats were drawn to this section due to the food lying around on the ground and, on occasion, a ferret was sent into their runs and terriers had a field day chasing the rats, which inevitably bolted. Feeding the pigs posed quite a problem, because whenever you had a bucket of swill to pour into the troughs, a dozen or so heads slammed in the way, whilst another six got between your legs and butted the bottom of the bucket, sending the slops all over you. One of my uncles who fed the pigs was very demure, quietly spoken and was always very polite, but on one particular such day, he lost his cool when becoming drenched through and after being thoroughly trodden on. He looked each way and then exploded with wrath and expletives only to be chastened in the extreme, when, above the din, he heard, "Good morning, Percy," from the watching vicar. He could have died from embarrassment!

Our Heritage

Further evidence of farm life can be deduced from the study of account books. Mr. J. R. Butler of Churchill Farm kept books for the first years of the twentieth century. Farming was more mixed in those days than now. Kale, potatoes, wheat, oats and barley were grown as was sugar beet after the opening of the factory in Kidderminster in 1925. Cattle, sheep and pigs were all bred on the farm. Mr. G. Butler can remember driving 150 sheep from Churchill to Warley Woods for summer pasture in 1918. He left at 5 a.m. and the journey took four hours up Hagley Hill and through Halesowen. There were few cars but lots of bikes, especially at the top of Mucklow Hill. One can imagine the chaos that would result from that happening today. The dipping of sheep in Churchill Mill Pool was also a common practice and very popular with children.

By 1912 a waggoner's wage had risen to 16/- per week and a cowman to 15/-. A rabbit catcher got 5/3d. for 10 rabbits, though a farmer received 14/- for selling them. The maid at the farmhouse was paid £1 per month but received board and lodging too. In 1912 two tons of potatoes from Blakedown were sold at Cardiff for £3, whilst six pigs were worth 17/6d. each.

It is interesting social history to notice which towns Mr. Butler visited in the course of a year. He had seven days holiday in Sussex in November, but closer at hand he visited Kidderminster several times, Bromsgrove for judging a number of times, Birmingham (twice), Worcester Fair, Bridgnorth, Warley Woods, Droitwich, Enville, Stewponey, Malvern Hills and London. There was also a trip to the circus, whilst hunting was a regular pastime.

Blakedown Honey Farm

In two other distinct ways the land has provided occupations for Blakedown people. Blakedown Honey Farm, Belbroughton Road, was set up by Mr. R. Bradford in 1950 and, after his death, was bought by Mr. R. May. It is now farmed solely by Mr. May and is one of the largest in the country with 600 hives in Herefordshire, Shropshire, Worcestershire and Staffordshire. From his Blakedown headquarters Mr. May travels some 50,000 miles a year bringing the honey back to be processed at Blakedown before it is sold all over the country.

from "A History of Churchill & Blakedown" by K J D Shabev - 1976

John Norman and Ethel Gertrude – My Parents

I am expecting my first great grandchild later this year, which will make the sixth generation of the family to be displayed on my sideboard photographs; not bad when we are only talking about the years 1921 through to 2006. At a friend's funeral recently, I discovered that she was 99 years old, and her two sons had given her a grand total of twenty-five great grandchildren (twenty-six this year) between them, which puts me to shame, as I cannot hope to compete with that – it takes two to tango as well as cooperation!

My father fought with the Worcestershire Yeomanry during the First World War and told us of many places where they were in conflict with the enemy; most of these places are now seen in our daily media. He travelled overland from the UK to the toe of Italy, where they boarded a ship for Alexandria. There was snow on the decks when they first boarded and by the time they reached Egypt, they could fry eggs on them. The horses were slung aboard with them and terrified neighs could be heard from up high in their slings as they were swept along by cranes. He fought the Turks in the Holy Land during most of the war years and their casualties were high and had to be supplemented by eighteen drafts later on. The Queen's own Worcestershire Hussars (when asked what QOWH stood for, the troops quipped, "The Quebec and Ontario wild horses!") sustained a larger number of casualties than any other British cavalry regiment on all fronts in the Great War.

My father used to talk of their exploits in Israel, Palestine, Iraq, and Egypt, and so the names keep reappearing with today's horrific stories of conflict. His commanding officer, Lord Cobham, from the Littletons of Hagley Hall, wrote a book of the war history of the Regiment, and my own father is mentioned within its contents, of which we, as children, were proud. He spoke of encampments in the desert where they had been surrounded by Bedouins, who used to beg for their horse manure, which they would dry out under the sun. With this, they would riddle out the unconsumed barley for their own food and cook it on the residual fuel. He said the regiment would embark on a 50-mile decamp in the middle of the night and their followers would catch up with them on foot the next morning. Even women in the middle of giving birth would only be a little delayed.

110 Record of Worcestershire Yeomanry – 1914–1922 by C. Lord Cobham

> During the afternoon of June 26th, a British airman dropped a message that three of his brother airmen had been shot down or forced to descend in the desert west of Khalassa, and that the machines were in need of immediate protection from Turkish patrols and scavenging Bedouins. The airmen had made good their escape to a cavalry advanced post at Basal. Soon after 5 p.m. the Regiment was on the move and rode 12 miles as quickly as possible across country. As darkness fell the Bedouins lit their customary warning bonfires, but beyond some light skirmishing with the advanced guard, during which Corporal Norman Butler of "A" Squadron had the satisfaction of pushing his sword through the back of a flying Turk at full gallop, there was no real opposition. Though the Regiment had been armed with steel for 123 years this is the first known occasion of its employment in battle by a member of it.

After WWI, he was offered some undeveloped land in Rhodesia, now called Zimbabwe, under a resettlement concessions scheme, but I am glad now that he stayed on and farmed back home, what with the whites being subjugated and losing all they ever owned and worked for, under a dictatorship.

In 1934, we moved from Churchill farm to Yieldingtree Farm. My father, who came from a long farming background, had nearly become bankrupted as swedes, which he had hoed tirelessly from 5.0 a.m. for days on end, had rotted with what is known as heart rot, his pigs had caught swine fever and had had to be slaughtered, his clovers had died presumably from a lack of lime and several horses had died in a row. One of the horses had ruptured itself whilst tipping potatoes into the clamp, another having developed a brain abscess and a further one having dropped dead between two others whilst ploughing. Each one had been a shire, weighing in at a ton a piece at a huge seventeen hands or more. With the added problem of blight ruining several potato crops, life was extremely hard after the Great Depression of the 1920s. The turn of the tide came in 1936, when fat lambs sold for more than they had cost in the autumn sales after fattening them for about four months. They cost about 14 shillings each and were sold for £2, what a welcome breakthrough that was!

My father was inclined to become frustrated and even somewhat aggressive towards the world around him if things didn't move as quickly as he liked or in the direction he thought best. He would help anyone out whom he thought needed a hand and would sometimes just give that help before being asked, occasionally resulting in his feelings being hurt if it was not appreciated or accepted in the way that it was intended. One such occasion was when he had helped out a friend, who had moved to another farm about 10 miles away by Bromsgrove. He had been harvesting and we had driven our horses and wagons over to help him out for several days. Father was most put out that he was not even thanked for his efforts at the end of it all, as the ungrateful friend told him he would have asked for help had he needed it; apparently, the friend had viewed it as interfering in affairs that didn't concern him.

During the war, some business friends turned up in the middle of the harvest and gave us a most welcome hand to haul the sheaves of corn to the barns. Being young and naive, I asked them in conversation what moved them to such generosity and love. They replied that my father had said come, and that in such circumstances, he was a man to be feared!

Driving a car brought out all the pent-up anger inside of him, as he could not bear to be behind another car at a distance of less than half a mile in front of him. At first sight, he would start to chunter and before long, his foot would be seen to be pressed hard down on the accelerator, with his bottom shoving backwards and forwards on the seat with grim frustration. He would shout, 'Get on, Liz; go on there,' until he had overtaken the first car, only to be exasperated by yet another one coming into view, with the prospect of it holding him up yet again. One day when Mother was aboard, he was driving up the high street in Kidderminster on the right-hand side of the road, when he had expostulated, because

Mother had pointed out his wayward ways when behind the wheel; his excuse being that with his vision and the foggy weather, he was getting her home the best he could under the circumstances, to which Mother said, "What fog?," which was when he realised that he had been wearing his reading glasses!

Another such example of his driving prowess was on our way to Borth for a week's stay as guests of Mrs Evans in 1936. We had crossed the main road at Wooferton in the direction of Presteigne and Knighton, when Mother had asked him to stop, as she needed to spend a penny. After a time, we passed a gateway and Mother had disappeared out of sight, only to return in extremis shortly afterwards, because she had sat on a stinging nettle. Whilst she was gone, another car had overtaken us, and as we had lost time, he turned his cap round and made a mad dash to overtake the car yet again.

Mother was amazing. On Sunday afternoons in particular, without so much as a fridge, we often had a horde of visitors to feed. I can never remember my mother going to church on a Sunday – only to marriages, christenings or funerals – her excuse being that she must get the dinner ready for us on our return. Even so, she was the most loving Christian woman who walked the earth. Everyone respected and loved her, as well as using her in a way; with relatives and friends just dropping in unannounced, in large numbers, often just before mealtimes, expecting to receive her hospitality in her own loving, graceful way.

If they stayed too late at night, Father would announce it was his bedtime and ask them to turn the light off on their way out, which usually did the trick.

Other visitors included reps, and one particular rep used to visit every Tuesday evening, often staying until very late. We called him Soapy Joe, until someone else unwittingly called him Mr Soap, which resulted in his visits being curtailed (I think he had matrimonial problems). Another rep was Mr Weavings, a great hit with us children. He always had a penny for us and told us many yarns and tricks that he got up to during his youth, generally when he was in his Austin Seven Ruby saloon. He used to travel for Jacksons corn merchants of Porters Mill, Droitwich way.

Then there was the local roadman, who had a progressive son, who later became a mechanic. He was lent some money to start up on his own, and, give old Joe Pardoe his dues, he was there at the drop of a hat at any hour of the day or night if he was needed, and always cheerful with it. He was a man who never forgot his lucky break in business and he more than repaid his gratitude, as seen in his long-standing service to the locals.

Mother was cautious of many old-fashioned legends and folklore, and forbade us to take snowdrops or elderflowers or suchlike into the house, for fear of it bringing bad luck. Beds must lie in the same direction as the floorboards, not across them. She was afraid of spooks or of anything bordering on the anti-Christ, and she believed that the parson could be the harbinger of ill tidings and must be treated with awe and respect, so as to not tempt the devil. Her mission in life was to protect, rear and love her family, and this she did with every sinew of her body and soul.

She slaved at keeping the big rambling farmhouse clean and tidy, our meals were always the best she could conjure up, and anything luxurious, such as strawberries and cream, overflowed on our own dishes, with only a modicum on her own. She would walk for miles to get something special for us, such as pork chops, and then scrub the quarry tiles on her hands and knees before we got in. Relatives came to stay for days at a time, often running into weeks or years, and they, in turn, found their haven in her care, along with the rest of us.

John & Ethel Butler (Nanny) at Broome Church

After a lifetime of virtual slavery, without ever having had a fridge, freezer or washing machine, she lived to the ripe old age of 93. Her last few years were not easy for her, her sight and hearing having declined over the years and her strength having left her, and even though we gave her all the help we could, she never deserved to just peter out like that. She was a wonderful woman, so loving, so loved, so kind, so respected, so gentle and so thoughtful of everyone, putting others' feelings before those of her own – we were privileged to have had such a mother, grandmother and great grandmother.

The War Years

The 'War Cry' came very suddenly: 'Your country needs you – grow more food, plough up your meadows and grow corn and potatoes. The ships are wanted for war work and are at high risk on the seas, your Duty calls.' But to do that, we needed labourers – land girls aplenty, school children for potato lifting (picking), tractors and new implements, trained men to drive them and, of course, money to pay for it all. Farmers had lived on the breadline through the depression years and had neither the money nor the confidence to branch out. The young men had left the land in favour of industry, and would not return to work the land again; in any case, few were trained to pick up the pieces. So the government, in turn, formed the War Agricultural Committees, with the power to force the ploughing up of meadows, thereby forcing unwilling farmers out. Discussion groups were formed to encourage farmers to comply, to engender competition for better yields.

The ploughing up of meadowland was compulsory if you were to grow wheat and potatoes. Horse-drawn binders emerged from rusting sheds and people converted to tractors, which were used to harvest 25–30 cwt crops of wheat per acre. Varieties included the long-strawed Little Joss and Yeoman, which flattened in the field and germinated when in the stooks when they matured for a week, before being hauled to the stacks or barns. Oats were popular then, too, and had to stand in the field stooks for three Sundays to prevent them from becoming hot, due to the knots in the straw. By cutting early and hauling late, it gave the straw good feeding qualities.

All plants were improved tremendously by the efforts of Sir George Stapleton at plant breeding stations, which were attached to universities, such as that in Aberystwyth, and in his case, carried an 'S' prefix, such as S24

Perennial Rye grasses, S147 Oats, S100 Clovers, S23 Cocksfoot, and S18 Timothy. These plant-breeding stations were also capable of producing heavier crops or shorter straw that stood up better at harvest time.

Potatoes posed a problem though, because, being a staple diet, they had to be stored in 'buries' or clamps (long, sunken troughs that had to be strawed over and soiled up to form sort of tents of about 50 to 100 yards long). School children were organised into groups to pick them up after the spinners had dug them up, and these would then be placed in boxes or sacks, which were hauled to the buries for storage. During the winter and in all weathers, they were then 'scovened' on to riddles, sorted into best and placed into pig sacks, where they were weighed and sent to market.

Sugar beet was also a highly intensive crop; from planting, we hoed them, singled them into seven-inch spaces, horse hoed them to maturity, pulled them up by hand, banged them together to help clean them, topped them individually by hand, and then tossed them into small heaps. They were then carted to heaps for the lorries using a hard surface for loading purposes, where they were 'scovened' yet again into the factory silos.

Riding horses was not my thing. I thought it was an expensive way to get uncomfortable and even injured. But my father, being an ex-cavalryman, used to go to the Birmingham Repository whenever the ex-cavalry-horse sales were on, and he would return with sturdy riding horses, which were strong enough to work on the lighter jobs, delivering on the milk round, crop hoeing, harrowing and the odd day's hunt on occasion. These horses were like sports cars in a way, and had minds of their own. Whilst driving the foxes out from the undergrowth, they milled around, but when a fox broke from cover and everyone else took off, they would stand stock still until the spirit and maybe the spurs said otherwise. If there was a railed fence with taller posts in between, they jumped the posts, sideways. To sit collected and calm when one charged into a wood, with low branches trying to decapitate the rider, took courage, and I often wondered whether the army selected the ones they thought might not hack the Battle of Balaclava for good reason.

Tommy was a treat in the float, and with his ears cocked forwards and toes clacking, he could go like the wind. Whenever he reached a white sign on the road, or manhole cover, he could swerve around without breaking stride. Having been tubed, with a valve inserted into his windpipe, as he was broken-winded, this used to make him roar as he sped along, causing some interested nosy parkers to turn heads.

The War Years

Bruce though was a devil. If you were harrowing and he saw anything resembling a jump, it was jumped. He also refused to pull in harness until his collar was warm, but this meant that the driver had to push the implement himself for the first ten minutes, and then hang on for dear life, as Bruce engaged gear and took off.

Another was a kicker, and if pulling a roller, she could beat a tattoo all day, and if on a hoe, could keep the front of it suspended for some time. We put her to the stallion and foaled, or covered, her as a means of taming her, but it never did. If she was in a field and took a dislike to something or other, she would charge with a great mouthful of teeth and then swing round and kick to high heaven; she should have been sent thence much earlier than she was. I won't give you her name – I think she must have been an orphan.

Sheep were fattened on the sugar beet 'tops' from netted pens laid out across the fields and the front wires were moved forwards each day the ten or so yards required. This meant their food was fresh everyday and the land manured evenly across the field for the following crops.

Cattle were reared and fattened in sheds and fed on mangold slices and chaff from the threshers, with some rolled corn on top. No wheat though; the country needed that for bread, and in any case it was prone to causing bloat and was detrimental to the horses especially.

Me on our Fordson Tractor in Wartime. Clent Hills in background.

Tractors were on 'strakes' or lugs' in the early days and used to cut up the road surfaces, so all the fuel, TVO (tractor vaporising oil), water and lubrication was carried to the fields in 5-gallon drums which got too heavy to carry after a quarter of a mile and more. They stayed in the field until their job was done; in the winter it was a job to start them each morning with the starting handles (no batteries or tyres back then). All sorts of ideas were hatched, such as making the plug leads jump a gap across a button, a squirt of ether, heating the plugs over a tin of petrol flames and retarding the ignition, amongst others.

At the start of the Second World War, wages for farm workers were 31 shillings and their tied cottage rent was deducted at 3 shillings per week. They usually had a large garden and potatoes and other farm produce was often available to them, in exchange for fifty to sixty hours work a week. On the other hand, the farmers themselves lived a similar lifestyle and as a child, who mixed, fed and played with the village children, I saw no difference between the diets in their cottages and those of our own farmhouse diets.

The farms had large amounts of staff to handle the workload and farmhouses were often huge, with cellars to match, because so many single employees lived in. The housewife carried a heavy workload, and was expected to clean, polish and maintain this edifice, on top of feeding cooking and laundering for the family, and four to six lodgers. There was no electricity or mains water, and no hot water, either.

A farmer's wife had a very hard life indeed. On wash day, staff in the wash house would have to fire up the copper, before pumping up the water from outside and bucketing it in. The dolly was then used to pound the suds through the clothes, and they would then be hung out on a clothes line, before using a flat iron heated on the hob to iron out the creases. In addition to this, she was expected to care for the chickens, carry the coals in and ashes out, not to mention the small matter of raising her family. If she got any help at all, it was usually from a girl who had just left school, who received a pittance for her hard labour. During the war years, the housewife was also expected to house evacuees and land girls.

The times of war meant many changes for all, from pre-war depression, wartime 'catching up' to stave off food shortages, home production following mass importing, the downgrading and upgrading of farms, dog and stick methods to escalated production, children's potato-picking parties, to machinery, and the ploughing-up of land orders. War

Agricultural Committees were set up, farms were graded and overseen – what a tremendous task! – dispossessions, supervision and advice given out to poorer farmers and farms, farmers' discussion groups, walks, talks and competitions the teaching of leadership and practicable methods, demonstrations, lectures and quizzes, and grassland being converted to arable were just some of the changes that these people saw. Staff shortages were filled up by the Women's Land Army, who had to acclimatise to outdoor life from offices and shops, from bathrooms to outside privies, from cold water pumps and taps to no running water, from cleanliness to grime and grind, and from city comforts and civilisation to a rural, run-down, poverty-stricken industry that was being encouraged to wake up and save the nation from starving at all costs. Ships were being sunk, all foreign imports had been stopped and the danger of being invaded was imminent, and call-ups meant a massive manpower shortage in all industries. What a tremendous upheaval!

During the war, farming was a reserved occupation. All possible efforts were made not only to do all your work as usual, but to 'do your bit' in other ways, too. Many joined the Local Defence Volunteers (LDV), later called the Home Guard, and every effort was made to become trained in warfare, to do sentry duties and guard installations, and to prepare defence posts. One had to learn intimately the lie of the land, so as to be most effective at night and to disappear from enemy view, in order to live to fight another day. Sleep was short after a night on duty and was sandwiched between normal work duties, catching forty winks whenever one could.

Service in the Home Guard meant, as with WVS (Women's Voluntary Service), fire watching, training for imminent invasions with forks for guns outside work hours, both at night and on Sundays, and the guarding of key installations, only to go back into work next day. The only day that one could relax was on market day, when one would prepare and sell livestock. Pea picking was a task requiring many hands. As with hop picking, it was the housewives that worked best when fast, selective handwork was needed.

It must be particularly hard to work out the economy of agriculture today, when not being actively involved. In 1980, wheat was sold for £110 per ton, and a new tractor cost say around £10,000; today, wheat only fetches £65 a ton and a new tractor costs £40,000–£60,000. Everything else seems to have escalated by similar proportions and ends don't seem to meet. Why should quotas be imposed on crops grown over here, when other people are going hungry around us? If land was planted with oilseed crops to produce diesel oil, would that not be better than paying (set aside) subsidies to keep land unproductive? Would that not be better than paying out huge sums to the Middle East for fuel oils? The object of joining the EU was to open up Europe for our exporting market, and to bring prosperity to the UK. However, it seems to be the case that most of the lorries which cross the Channel seem to be on one-way trips, returning empty to say, Spain, to collect yet more vegetables to bring back here. Even our holidaymakers are going abroad for their holidays and buying houses over there; not only that, but all the meat supplied to our own army is from South America. Milk quotas have been cut, whilst at the same time, we are importing tankers of milk from the continent. This is giving out such confusing messages to our younger members of the land that they are now looking for careers overseas, and who can blame them?

It was always said that farmers were only needed during wartime, as we needed to export our industry's products to the empire, taking cheaply produced feeding stuffs in payment. Now our empire has evaporated, we are facing the same depression, as seen in the closure of our factories and the buying-in of goods produced in the east, where the wages are so low that we cannot even hope to compete at home, but what does the future hold if this process continues? If there was war tomorrow, as a country, we would hardly be self-sufficient.

Our ancestors would only buy an article if they could pay cash for it, and as young couples they were thrifty and would build a nest egg for their union, with one piece of furniture at a time whenever they could afford it, or they would be given or would inherit a second-hand piece. Nowadays, a newly-wed expects to start out in life with the same type of house as it took their own parents a lifetime to acquire; with all the gadgets, freezers, TV, videos, CDs, microwaves, washing machines, central heating, car and such like to go with it. On top of this, they want to 'buy' a new house to go with it all. To pay for this way of life, they live in cloud cuckoo land, using plastic cards, hire-purchase agreements, mortgages and insurances, all of which leave them in debt for life. At least, I suppose, they are able to reap the benefits as they toil through life, whereas our predecessors toiled through life just to get the benefits!

A farmer friend of mine, Arthur Pardoe from Stone, was ploughing by tractor with a trailed two furrow plough one day. As there was rather a lot of rubbish going under the plough and hanging on to the body of it, he stepped off the Fordson without stopping it (as was often the case). He tried to clear the plough frame whilst it was in motion, but, unfortunately, his foot became caught in the furrow, throwing him over on his back and snapping his leg with a loud crack. He was unable to free his leg, and he was dragged to the end of the furrow, through the hedge and across the next field. Charlie Jones was horse ploughing at the time and had seen what was happening. Leaping into action, he stopped the engine, extracted the limb and lifted Arthur on to the horse's back, but the foot pooled with blood like a bucket, and the pain was too excruciating for him to bear. They got him down and he held on to the harness, with his foot dragging against the floor, until they eventually reached home. An ambulance took him to hospital, where a surgeon said that amputation was the only answer, but Arthur said he was born with it and would die with it, and would not allow any severance. Thanks to the skills of the staff in the hospital, he recovered, and without even so much as a limp.

Arthur's daughter, Thelma, married a GI and after moving to America, Arthur and Hattie went to visit them some years later, but had a lot of trouble getting a passport. It appeared that the wetting of the baby's head must have got out of hand, because his birth certificate had him down as Martha and no one had even noticed. He had to be medically examined and guarantees had to be given that he had not had an operation before he had obtained his visa. One can imagine the hilarity of the event by his contemporaries when it all got out, especially as he was chairman of the District Council and War Agricultural Agent, and so well known to boot – the papers had a heyday!

Arthur's son, also called Arthur, was my best man. Arthur went virtually straight from school into the Spitfires over London, and could fly a Spit through the eye of a needle. To break the rules, Arthur thought it great sport to fly under bridges and on one occasion, returned to base with cables and wires hanging from his rudder, which were a great cause for concern for the maintenance staff awaiting his arrival, as they were like whips cracking down the runway. One of only a few Spitfire pilots, he also rested in Canada for a while, training new pilots, before being sent to the Far East, where he flew the new wooden Mosquito. They lost so many comrades who never returned to base that it bugged him throughout his life. He married my sister Betty in later years, who was in the WAAF, and after the war he farmed at Cleobury Mortimer.

Another of his sagas in life included doing the victory roll with his Singer car – this upset many of his passengers, and meant hosing out the car on several occasions! On another occasion, he was driving up a long and twisty lane at home when he had a nervous passenger, who expostulated at the ridiculous momentum of their progress. Arthur told him not to be so jittery, he could do it in a lot less time with a few pints inside him, but this was no comfort to the passenger, who objected even more. Arthur snatched the steering wheel off the column and handed it over to him with a, 'Here then – you drive!' Needless to say, the car had to be hosed out again!

When the clocks were put forward into 'double' summer time (clocks were put forwards by two hours rather than one to give a longer working day) my father said no one was going to tell him when to get up and refused to alter the clocks; just imagine the confusion of everyone having to work out what time the buses ran, or the market started, or when the agent was due to appear each day. He stuck it out for quite some time, until mutiny, despair and threats forced the issue.

My father had an old Austin Seven car at the outbreak of war for economy purposes, and this had a folding canvas top, with perspex windows which lifted out, and he insisted on delivering the woolsacks to town on top of this poor little car. The woolsacks were huge and when placed across the car, they stuck out by about 3 feet on either side, leaving the driver seated with his nose against the steering wheel; in fact, the sacks were as big as the car itself, and Father could never understand why Mother refused do her shopping on the same visit, even though it meant her screwing down into the footwell for half the journey. It certainly was a wonderful motor though, and only cost around £24; as well as shopping and woolsack runs, it was also expected to carry loads of up to half a ton of vegetables on the back seat when needs must.

Another old car he bought for £40 was a square-built Hillman of about 14 hp, which had a gate-change gearbox and needed a double-declutch to get going. However, a little hinged gadget prevented the lever from going into reverse, except that it was missing in our case, and whenever we were in a queue of traffic, say at traffic lights, for example, it was amazing how the cars behind reacted when 'green' light shone and all except us started forwards. Instead, we went backwards, and side windows were wound down for expostulation and horns made a cacophony of sound around us, whilst Father just said, "Damn", and never even seemed to notice – woe betide an errant driver who cut him up though.

In 1939, on a wet day, my father decided we would have a day out and go to the Royal Show at Windsor Park, but in the middle of Oxford, the Hillman cut out at the traffic lights and refused to start. It had no electric starter and the crank handle was swung with much vigour and vengeance. When the light turned to green, all hooters blared, and after a few further light changes, we pushed the vehicle over to the other side and away it went, but not unnoticed by rather a lot of people by that time. By the time we arrived, a couple of policemen were running through the throng with a rope each to open up a corridor for the royal family (King George VI of England, the queen and two princesses). We could have shaken hands with any one of them that day as they passed us by. Princess Elizabeth, of course, would have been thirteen years old then, and now, as Queen Elizabeth, she is eighty later this year. How time flies.

A short while ago I received a telephone call from the police, asking me what I had done with the bomb in the 'channels' in 1942, to which I replied that I had ploughed it in! The fact was that a bomb had been dropped or jettisoned there during a raid over Birmingham in 1942, and it had left a hole in the field about 3-foot wide and 6-foot deep, without exploding, but as to how far down it penetrated, I have no idea, as a covering of soil blocked the view. Being young and supposedly ploughing this field for potatoes, I asked my father what to do about it. He thought that if the authorities came to dig the bomb out, it could be some weeks wasted, and it was time to get the land prepared now. His reaction was to, 'say nowt and fill the hole in', so I ploughed the ground until it was level, and then we prepared the tilth and planted the potatoes. Whatever it was is still there to this day, and it was only because a new bypass was planned to be built nearby that my brother happened to mention the matter some years later. He was still a schoolboy of 12 years at the time, but is now the farmer and sends Shakerater cultivators over the very spot which could, I suppose, ignite the thing. The new road scheme seems to have been diverted or cancelled, so may it rest in peace forever. The hedges denoting the exact position have now gone, and I am sixty-four years older than I was then, but I am confident that I could near enough pinpoint the spot to this day. I guess there must be other similar situations around the country, where roads or buildings have been constructed, which could have been disruptive, eruptive, or very frightening.

Highway to Destiny

When the bomb disposal teams were busy in Coventry, we were shown pictures in the newspapers showing the men sitting on bombs, that had been dug up and were now resting on the back of lorries, eating their lunch and sometimes being held up at traffic lights in a queue – what nerves those teams must have had, and what a risky job of making them safe and of getting them out. Heroes all.

Kidderminster YFC Judging Team - 1944 - County & Individual Cups

Wartime Home-Guard Incidents

One of our earlier duties was to guard the Axborough Water Reservoir and to observe the skies from there for parachutists entering the region as spies. The reservoir was in the centre of a thickly planted forest and was fairly high up: under the canopy of branches it was as black as night and the pathway was narrow with ferns and briars rubbing against your legs.

With one man on guard and two asleep at any one time, it was a bit creepy, as someone with evil intent had only to stand still and club you as you passed him. With this in mind, when a rabbit bolted in the undergrowth a yard away, it made you jump to it rather smartly.

One night, when I was the lone ranger, I walked the 200-yard track to the road entrance when I heard footsteps approaching in the distance. Knowing I was invisible if standing still, I waited until the figure passed by and then as sharply as possible, shouted, "Halt," hoping to scare the person to death. Instead of the expected result, I, in turn, was answered by a passing drunk, demanding to know if I was the 'B***' who ran over his legs two nights before!

I had heard that that particular night the guard on duty had, indeed, run over a drunk's legs, as he sat in the grass verge with his legs across the road, but he had failed to stop, owing to the urgency of the hour. This same drunk was hopping mad and ready to storm the parapets and I was mighty glad when he decided to let it be and stagger on his way.

Our platoon was a mobile unit and could be sent to wherever it was needed in an emergency, unlike most other units, and were to be our invisible army, attacking at night, before disappearing into the night again. It was my duty to transport our chaps to wherever sent and in whatever transport was available at the time. One Sunday, we were to join the 'Company' at the Kidderminster sugar-beet factory for inspection, where we were expected to excel at marching and other manoeuvres, in order to show off our prowess. The order came fairly suddenly and the only lorry I could requisition was our own farm lorry, which had been handling messy manure all week and hadn't yet been cleaned off. Imagine the consternation when polished shoes and pressed-uniformed guards were told to climb aboard! The sides of the bed were fairly shallow and everyone tried to stand up to try and stay clean, until we got under way at a fair lick, that is, which imposed a safer method of travel, but an enraged platoon on arrival were ready to lynch the driver (me) for them turning out for inspection in such a state. (A bit like Wurzell Gummage one might add, only smellier.)

Another time we were to repel an enemy moving in from Bridgnorth, and we spent the night in a wood near Shatterford. It was cold and wet and most uncomfortable out in the open with the only cover being that provided by the trees. We were supposed to be getting a supply of blankets and some drinks sent round, but they never reached us. We heard later that the only blankets available totalled three, and as there were not enough for the platoon to share, the NCO slept under them himself; I suppose he must have drunk the tea, also. As well as being cold and wet, we were eaten alive by midges that night, too, but pleased to learn the next day that the invasion had swerved off on the opposite side of the river.

Our early days were rather pathetic, as we had no uniforms or arms for some time. We practised with broom stales for rifles and studied aircraft recognition, map reading and other military training, before we were eventually issued with WWI rifles and Mills grenades, which had been stored in America in cases of axle grease. These were de-gunged, cleaned up and given out, at which point we all had to memorise our number and see whether the equipment still worked whenever ammunition came along in dribs and drabs. We practised bayonet drill and on the 'thrust', we let out a blood-curdling yell, which was taken up on one occasion by a flock of peacocks, loud enough to have wakened the dead and scared off any ghost or lurking individual.

Later still, we had to take our turn at guarding the tunnels at Drakelow near Wolverley. These tunnels were an underground factory for Rover, the car manufacturer, and were said to be seven miles long in the direction of Kinver, and only a short distance from the prehistoric caves, which are now listed and have just been sold for a £100,000. We were not allowed into the complex though, which was secret and off limits to everyone.

During the early hours, a nurse was to be collected and escorted to her billet a little way off, and I was given the task of escorting her. Everyone wanted to know what she looked like and how old she was, and I gave a very promising description of a 20-year-old blonde, with an hourglass figure and lovely, smiling nature, which went down well, but was far from the truth.

The blessing of that task was that I gained access to the complex, which was awe-inspiring in that the walls and roof were cut from the red sandstone rock without any lining. The roof must have been about 30 feet in height and width, and the straight lengths were joined by cross tunnels, making it seem like an enormous underground enterprise. After the war, it was set up as a nuclear shelter for government officials, and is now a disused 'has been', albeit a credit to our engineers at a time of great need in desperate wartime conditions.

One of the excitements of those days was when we were instructed in the art of throwing live grenades, with seven-second fuses, and someone accidentally dropped one on the floor amongst our feet, with the fuse still burning. An officer quickly grabbed it and tossed it clear before any harm came to us, but it certainly concentrated the mind of us part-time country soldiers.

We were also issued with Blacker Bombard mortars, which we loaded with black powder and then a bottle of phosphorous, before shaking it down the sloping barrel and firing it at the supposed enemy. Invariably, the bottle burst and the thing was more dangerous to the user than any enemy, as it splashed fire and acid in all directions.

Another stupid idea was a bomb like a small football, with a saucepan-like handle. The ammo was wrapped in ladies' stockings and covered with hen manure, and its intended use was to let enemy tanks pass over us, at which point we would stick them on to the underbelly, before we were squashed by the tracks. I've no doubt we could have been a nuisance to an invading force, but the German answer to us would have been mass slaughter of the nearest villages. This had been the price paid by others before us who delayed the advancing hordes. Thank goodness it never got that far in Britain, but we all knew the cost of being overrun and dominated by the Nazi regime, and we were prepared to take our chance, as in a nest of wasps when disturbed.

Dad's Army is a very amusing television series to watch, but it was in actual fact quite true to life and the times, only then things were taken much more seriously at a time of our history when we were very vulnerable to a well-trained and armed invading enemy, who, up till then, had swamped all before it.

Alice

The Women's Land Army (WLA) was an invaluable service and many girls became very skilled workers, and although they were originally townsfolk, they often stayed on the land, marrying countrymen, Alice included. Voluntary work became a must everywhere, and included fire watch duties, phone operators, plane spotters, WVS social workers and so on.

Finding a wife, who supports and encourages you, whilst advising you of your errant ways when necessary, is wonderful and stimulating. It is a fortunate man who finds and loves such a girl, and he is all the more fortunate when blessed with a long life together, as we were, especially if the marriage is fruitful and someone is brought up to follow in your footsteps and to help you in old age. Did you give them time, love and friendship enough when you were busy and they needed you? Mother did! But Father, striving to prosper, never gave enough.

My girlfriend, Alice, became my wife. She had also joined the WLA to do her bit in the war. She was studying to be a speech therapist at the time,

Highway to Destiny

but was unable to get time off to pass her final exam to qualify. She came from a respected family of farming butchers and his father (along with her brother and sister) ran a dairy business in Hoylake, also selling home-made ice cream – made with 2 dozen eggs, butter, sugar, 2 gallons of fresh cream, etc. – home-made jams and so on.

Car tyres were in short supply during the war, and we were all driving around with the white canvas showing, where a good tread is now the law. I once went to visit my girlfriend, Alice, in Clitheroe, who was recovering from a physical breakdown from her land army work and possibly from some effect or other from the arsenic crop sprays she used to use on the apple orchards. The tyres were all showing white and the spare was off a motorbike. Anyway, the day turned out to be hot and lifted the patches on the repaired tyres. About eleven punctures and thirteen hours later, I arrived on her doorstep worn out and somewhat worse for wear, and missed the local show, thereby causing great concern to all! We drove back in the pouring rain, with no spare tyre and no stops, the following day in three hours. What a marathon journey that was though.

Courting was hard work in those days, and owing to the lack of petrol coupons, a bike was the answer. I never liked bikes – they found aches and muscles that I never knew I had. Just to see Alice meant biking 6 miles, and to take her out to the pictures involved a further ten miles or more on bad roads. Another complication was her land army friend Olive, who insisted that as she knew Alice first, she must come along also. If we managed to squeeze in a walk by ourselves, Father insisted that we exercised the bull at the same time. Now what chance has a lad for a cuddle with his girl on one hand and a fractious bull on the other? But with the long working days plus our war work, even being able to meet up was a bonus. Alice produced charity events and plays in Chaddesley Corbett in her spare moments from threshing six days a week with the contractor Trevor Pardoe, or hoeing beet, as called upon, with the Merediths. In the spring, she was sent out spraying fruit trees in the Teme Valley, with dinitro-ortho-cresol, arsenic or other noxious sprays under high pressure being used.

Alice

Alice's grandfather's butcher's shop c.1900, prior to its demolition. His new replacement Webster Building seen behind at Padiham

Cousin George was a skilled (apprenticed) carpenter like his father before him, but after having contracted 'walkabout fever', he joined the French Foreign Legion after going AWOL from the army. Because of having served in another army, he escaped punishment from going AWOL – this is considered an offence as a soldier, and he would thus have broken his vows to his monarch in doing so. We met him as an itinerant carpenter in Umtali, Rhodesia, in the 1960s.

Because Alice's parents were of different churches, Alice was at home in the Anglican and Methodist faiths and was a very committed Christian throughout her life. We were married in St Paul's Church (Church of England) in Clitheroe on 8 May 1946, and were devoted to each other for sixty years, before she died. A marriage made in heaven, I was 22 and Alice 24 at the time. The first of our children, Rozanne, was born 2 June 1947 at Bellington, Harvington in Worcestershire.

Michael John was born 24 April 1949, at Rock, Worcestershire.
Robert was born 22 October 1953, at Rock, Worcestershire.
Bridget Mary Macie was born 21 December 1964 at Maciene, Mozambique.

Grandchildren:
from Ro – Andy and Emma, with Gordon
from Mike – twins, AJ and Nick, with Eiola
from Rob – Sarika with Kathy
from Bid – Chillie and Livvie-Rose, with Paul

Great Grandchildren:
from Nick – Charlie, with Kate.

Married life involved working at home where sixty-hour weeks earned a farmer's son a princely £6 a year including, board and lodging and clothing, to being suddenly expected to manage a farm and make all the decisions – planning, hiring and firing, book work, stockman, arable enthusiast, weather predictor, disease and pest recogniser and treater, barrow boy, entrepreneur, vet, labourer and being responsible for taking the buck, all whilst showing a profit and still being a friend and trusted by those around you – is a big jump and can be intimidating, though with the bliss of youth it can also be enjoyable and demanding.

Alice was special. I loved her from our first sight and the feeling was mutual for sixty years.

Alice muck spreading - 1944

We fought God to give up our home, our farm, and future as we saw and planned it, and we thought we had lost to Him, but He gave us our most wonderful years; the memories of those wonderful years in Africa made us truly grateful to Him. We never expected or visualised the future in His hands, working His vineyard, but they were the most stimulating and satisfying years of a long life together. We knew we would have no pension to look forward to, we knew that what little money we had would dissolve as indeed it did, due to the expenses being greater than the financial reward, but we believed that if we were asked to do His work, we would be looked after in the future, as we so often have been.

We returned home back to the UK eventually, with only a second-hand car to our names, and we made our home in Wales, where prices were lower and we prospered. Yes, we made mistakes, but we survived. We tried to make Sundays a day for church and animals, but not for work. We saw our family grow and start successful lives and businesses, and we, Alice and I, shared a heaven-sent marriage for almost sixty years, before she was called for her reward. She had a long and miserable illness at the end, although she never complained, and nor would she, and now she has gone, she has inspired a lazy me to record some of our experiences for the children and any others who may be interested.

At this point, I feel compelled to write down some moving events from her passing. Rozanne and I had arranged the funeral leaflets and had organised the details for the service, before preparing for bed at about 11.0 p.m. the night beforehand. The Teasmade then made us a cup of tea to go to bed on, and yet no one had even switched it on. Were the arrangements acceptable? At the end of the service, before leaving the church for the interment, I told the packed church how Alice had been broken-hearted a week before her death. She had dreamt that she was at her own funeral and that no one had come, and all about how she had sobbed, "No one loves me any more," so I thanked everyone for the hundreds of cards and for filling the church, telling them that Alice would now know that she is loved and that we do care. When the candles were extinguished, the centre candle of a three-branch candelabra had burnt to the base, the others remaining as new. Had she heard us? At the graveside, Ro read the poem *Do Not Stand at My Grave and Weep*, and a butterfly had encircled her head; was it she? How Great Thou Art!

On the first anniversary of her death, I was at the Sunday service; the same candle went out as I thought of her. The following year, I was not well enough to go to church and Holy Communion was brought to me at home; when her name was mentioned, the same left-hand candle went out.

Bellington

I became the manager of Bellington and lived there until our marriage in 1946. Bellington was a beautiful old timbered house of sixteenth-century origin and had been, I believe, a coaching house in its past history, although it is a show house for moguls these days.

Bellington

At milking times, the owner, Mr Mole, an industrialist, would sometimes ring up to request the cows being milked in the parlour be cleaned up and with tails fluffed out to demonstrate his prowess to his business friends, visiting at 4.30 p.m. With the machines already ticking away milking like clockwork, by the time they eventually pitched up in their

Bentleys at 4.45 p.m., we had already moved on to the next batch of cows, only for them to see these ones that had not yet been refined, and with a now dirty floor. With cows getting nervous from a broken discipline and with strangers about, it seemed to give them the mighty gift of the runs. The 'pinstripes' were not pleased by such a splashy reception, the manure being whisked far and wide by the cows' tails acting as distributors, and who got the blame?

Passing up on the interest of the Farmers Discussion Group was sorely missed, on my part, as we had started getting the annual show going again and competition was fierce. Other than the usual debates, we organised visits to the most progressive farms along with the War Agricultural Committee, we organised demonstrations of machinery coming on to the market and we gave talks on the new varieties of cereals out, in addition to giving out information concerning general methods of up-to-date husbandry.

Running alongside these events, I had also been very involved with the Young Farmers Club at Kidderminster from its inception in about 1940 and this gave a lot of instruction to us in similar activities. Being of a younger age, we were also taught the art of public speaking, cattle-judging, bee-keeping, poultry and egg-production, hedge-laying, sheep-breeding and so on. The stress of this industrialised 'Mole' farming was high, and at twenty-two to twenty-three years of age, and being newly married, we decided to move on. We had shown a profit for the first time for Mr Mole and the bonus earned was slashed by income tax and costings, which reduced it to pence per hour anyway, so away we went to Whytehouse Farm to start off on our own, Alice and I.

My first insight into other people's affairs came when Mr Mole sued his wife for divorce in Birmingham High Court, and I was subpoenaed to appear by my boss to prevent his wife from doing likewise. Four days of sitting in the outer passage was a bind, but as I was being paid to do so it eased the pain somewhat. He later employed two widows as housekeepers and as I was living in at the time, I was often called in to help out. One day, they were decoking the Aga and could not get it restarted, and thus sought my help. Not realising that the innards of the Aga were now hot from their efforts, I promptly relayed the firebox with paper, sticks, and charcoal, tipped some paraffin over it, held a match to it and closed the doors. The next thing we knew, the paraffin vaporised and exploded with a heck of a bang. The door of the Aga flew open, the heavy rings on top flew up in the air and the place was smothered in heavy smog before we knew where we were. We groped our way to the door and were met by a crowd of running workers, who had heard the bang and had seen the smoke go up. Needless to say, against all orders to the contrary, the housekeepers concerned never again decoked the Aga – I suppose it wouldn't have needed it for quite a while in any case, perhaps even several years after that event.

One man called Clogger who worked with us was always game for a laugh. He was called-up during the war and after his first leave, returned to his duties in his friend's plus fours and a bowler hat, having sold his rifle and uniform for beer money. The army's way of disciplining him for this was for him to fill a drain in the middle of the parade ground with water from a far-off tap. After three days, he mutinied, as, in his words, 'it would never overflow'. When working on a corn stack, he always used to try to lift the sheaf of corn he was standing on, and the long fork handles resembled fishing rods. Clogger specialised in cleaning out the old earth closets, and the story went that at one particular farm they caught him stirring the smell (?) with a long stick. When the farmer complained about the awful smell, he said he had dropped his jacket in, to which the farmer replied, "Stop and I will find you an old jacket." 'It's not only that,' said Clogger, "my lunch is in the pocket!" Another thing he used to say was that the pubs did not make him welcome in those days, and he complained that it was impossible to get his boots clean to gain entry, if they were too mean to leave a broom by the door.

Our herd at Bellington was of Ayrshires, based on the Lessnessock and Bargower herds, which yielded a good butter fat percentage, which was the order and price basis of the day. The vogue changed over the years though, and the Friesians won popularity. The Friesian cow was bigger and her yield was higher, but we referred to them as water milk cows. To give you an idea, the rough yields and fats of the day were as follows:

Friesians	1,200 gallon	@ 2.9–3% BF
Ayrshires	800–1000 gallon	@ 4%
Jerseys	700–800 gallon	@ 5%
Horses		@ 6%
Sheep		@ 6%

Nowadays, with less physical work, we eat less fatty food and the adverts are not for 4% butterfat milk, but labelled 'our milk is 96% fat free'. These days, because the carcass of the Friesian is bigger, it is crossed with Belgian Blue, Simmental, Blonde D'Aquitane and Charolais bulls, in order to get double-muscled fattening stock, with the calves being exported for the veal trade or fattened here for bigger beef. The Hereford lost a lot of ground to these breeds, because they were smaller bred than before and are not double-muscled. For the Argentine ranches, the Herefords proved to be very popular and with their dark eyelids, they could withstand the very bright sunlight. The Jerseys are kept pure though, because the Island will not import outside lines and as they are usually tethered or in small herds, they suit the needs at home. Farming goat's milk is a risky business though, as it can smell at certain times of the year (as is the case with sheep's milk), but it is said to be TB free.

Cheeses differ widely and Cheddar is produced throughout the world. I personally like the Cheshire Red, because it is a dry, crumbly cheese, but the choices now range from smooth and creamy to strong, matured goat, sheep and cow's cheese, with pre-packed cheeses from many exporting countries, such as the continent, and New Zealand, as well as home-grown produce.

When the Chaddesley Farmer's Club was revived in 1942 after many years of disbandment, I, as a stripling, was asked to be secretary and this post was kept up until I took my first job with Mr Mole at Bellington, who insisted that one could only serve one master. Mr Mole, with his brother, were Birmingham industrialists making, amongst other things, the Mole self-grip wrench. His only knowledge of farming was that of what he read in the *Farmers Weekly*, concerning what was done on their own farms; this, he computed against industrial practices and modes, and percentages of labour costings versus output were a favourite with him. This concept was all new to me though, as to spend hours hoeing a crop, taking into account its relative costs, did not necessarily mean a cost plus price for the article on the farm, especially if that article was fed to a cow, and became a part cost of the milk for only a short time of the year, which could even be during the cow's dry period, or at her most productive cycle anyway.

The Young Farmers' Club was formed in order to get modern education in agriculture for the youths, which was lacking at the time, because of the depression years, with a lack of money, machines and technology. YFC experiences included stock-judging, public speaking, the visiting of large progressive farms and demonstrations by War Agricultural Committees. Sir George Stapleton's lectures at Aberystwyth, Bangor and Drayton, Stratford-on-Avon are memorable. I myself was the third chairman of Kidderminster YFC and we won several cups in various county competitions.

After farming at Bellington for a time and getting married, we went on to farm on our own account at the Whytehouse at Rock, which was a steep, heavy-clay farm, compared to the easier arable loams of Bellington. It was a challenge, but at least we had started out on our own.

Whytehouse Farm

The Whytehouse was sometimes depicted by the War Agricultural Committee as adopting a progressive form of farming. From our Young Farmers' Club training and outlook, we tried to go with the flow and the status of the farm was raised from a grade C to grade A in a remarkably short space of time.

Whytehouse Farm

One of the interesting things which came out of this phenomenon was the farm walks organised by the War Agricultural Committee, and we were even visited so that others could see our methods of silage-making for themselves, and this led on to an organised visit from France. We were over the moon to see what sort of girls the French could produce, as they were reputed to be so wonderful, so pretty, so petite and such good cooks to boot. Well, they weren't bad either, but their boyfriends were a real let-down. How could such men produce such pretty girls? However, when we walked the farm and notepads came out, questions flew from all sides as to the mixtures of seeds in each meadow, the amount and analysis of all fertilisers for each different crop and the analysis and feed per gallon for the different yielding cows. To give them an interest, I asked someone with a 20-ton bulldozer doing some work for us to push over a big sycamore tree, which was a nuisance in the centre of a field. Its roots were wide and shallow and it took a huge amount of effort to remove it, by which time tears were flowing and I was, I'm sure, an ogre!

A neighbour's wife inherited their own small farm and her husband, being a miner, came to farm it. He was a most unhappy soul, as he put it, and working in a mine, crawling half a mile to the coalface with eighteen inches of headroom was far preferable to farming. At least in the mine the temperature was the same every day, and all you were expected to do was to lie on your side and hack at the coal, and on Friday, you knew you would get paid for your work.

With the farm, you were out in all weathers, all hours, day and night, suffering from every pest imaginable, often bearing a loss, and at the year's end, you offered your hard-won produce to markets, with a plea for offers, rather than cost plus to survive on. He was also affected by the moon's changes, and was known to try to open his front door with an axe in the early hours, when the door was not even locked. His wife went berserk one day when she had just finished the spring cleaning and he decided to sweep the chimney. His method was to drop a rope down the chimney from above, with a holly bush attached to the other end of it. Only on this occasion, the bush jammed on the way down and was too tight to dislodge. He extended the rope through the house and tied it to a horse, and a sharp smack on the animal's buttocks sent it off at quite a pace. The offending bush came down at speed and along with it, smoke, dust and cobwebs, straight through the house, leaving a trail of debris in its wake.

An elderly neighbour had built a house for his retirement nearby and had asked myself and an old sage to come and admire the finished article that he was so proud of. The old sage sniffed a bit and paced about, measuring up with his size ten boots here and there, and then said, 'I don't like it; your landing is too narrow and your bedroom doors too ockerd to get a coffin out'. For an elderly man's retirement home it did seem a bit frank! Needless to say, we were deprived of the whiskey that had been laid out for us and we were given short shrift to the door.

Whytehouse Farm

Our life together at the Whytehouse Farm, Rock, was one big adventure. We built cow sheds and bull pens and even installed a Rayburn in the house for hot-water supplies. The pastures were reseeded to better leys of modern grass mixtures, even including herbs in some. Fences were made stock proof and presentable, and the gates were made to swing on hinges, without being tied up with string. Hens were initially tried in back-kitchen batteries, before a change was made to loft-deep litter pens. Berkshire sows were allowed to pig outdoors, and the piglets were only weaned at eight weeks. Berkshires are excellent grazers and do well, but are inclined to run to fat and lost popularity to the Landrace, which was not as hardy, but had a higher percentage of lean meat. We tried to be as self-sufficient as we could, but with aim of high output, it became necessary to buy in more and more proteins and pre-prepared, balanced stock feed.

With dodgy summers and haymaking problems, the machinery to make silage improved and was a more reliable feed. But as the years went by we changed from full-length grass silage to chopped, and then double chopped, which was easier again both for us and also for the cattle, as it enabled them to get sufficient intake and a longer period of rest and cudding time. Instead of them trying to pull a meal from a tight wall face of silage, they could now lap it up from the floor or manger.

Likewise, over the years, the milking chore has altered. In the 1930s, hand milking meant one man to eight cows, and then gradually new ideas came along for machine milking. Then along came the 6 x 6 parlours, where one man now stood upright to attach the milking cups, via the Roto parlours. And from here, came the 12 x 6, and now the 16 x 32 parlours, where one man is able to milk 300 cows by himself, what a jump in technology!

These days, every cow has a numbered tag, and/or a freeze-branded hindquarter number. When the cow enters the parlour, a computer gives her a rationed amount of grain, the milk is stored in tanks and the cows go into open cubicles. The milk is then collected the next day by a milk tanker. The bull has been replaced by Artificial Insemination done by the herdsman, and the manure goes into lagoons and is piped out to the fields. Is this factory farming, too? When a large staff was employed and one went sick, the others took the strain, but these days, when a couple of men run 600 acres and one goes sick, life becomes much harder, with serious consequences.

The Parish of Rock was also a fruit-growing area, and orchards of cherries, damsons and blackcurrants were prevalent. These days, they have all gone, the trees grubbed out with the hedges, with corn growing in their place, whilst we import our cherries from Italy instead. Even the small dairy herds have gone, and the combine has taken over. Economics have forced production to specialised businesses, one such example being that the farmyard chickens are now housed in crowded pens in large sheds, where 40,000 to 200,000 birds are cared for by two people and lots of gadgets. Henry Ford certainly started a trend with his mass production methods and robots all those years back.

One of our pioneering endeavours was dehorning the herd of mature cows, and later calves, so that they could be housed in the winter in open yards, without damaging one another. This was fine at home, but, as with TB-free herds of that time, the pioneers had no outlet markets, as it was some years away from being the norm, and eventually, compulsory. I remember the cows having to be anaesthetised one day, and we had to help the vet lop the horns off the animal near to the skull using a large sort of pruning shear. The arteries spurted a jet of blood about 8 feet into the air, and we dabbed a wad of cotton wool into the cavity that had been left behind. This sometimes came out, and one particular individual, who was coming down the drive at the time, on being confronted by emerging cows and jets of blood, fell off his bike in horror. The jets soon stopped though and healed up well, but those with wads became infected under the resulting scab and we had to pull the wads out with cork screws. From then on, all calves at a week of age were treated with a caustic pencil on their horn buds, which proved effective, but was later replaced when compulsory regulations came in, when the bud was burnt off with a gas-heated disbudder; personally, I preferred the caustic pencil.

Rothamsted Experimental Station, a Government college, broke the four-course farming system by proving that corn could be grown for one hundred years in succession, with the right fertilisers and weed sprays. Previously, the third corn crop had never been very good, and it would appear that that was due to a disease build up, which outgrew in later years when it became more controllable. During the war and later, crop yields were bred into corn varieties, so that the wheat and barley yields rose from 1 ton per acre to 4 tons, and with shorter straws they could carry the weight without going flat and becoming spoiled before the harvest.

The pole elevator was another interesting haymaking gadget. When the sweep became popular and a field of hay was swept into a central point, the pole was set up with a slight lean towards the rick. A swinging boom could transverse 100 degrees or so, and a rope was fastened to a large grab and led down to a bottom pulley. This was then led out to a horse and on the word go, the horse went forwards for 20 to 30 feet, lifting the grab full of hay, which swung up and over the rick, where a cord trip dropped it. The horse then reversed for the next grab, whilst the rick builder sorted out the deposited load. This gadget was eventually supplemented by an elevator, which was engine driven, but less ingenious. A large hay knife was used to cut out bundles of hay keitches during the winter (a bit like a bale, only it wasn't tied up) where it was then carried to the feeding racks. The early balers delivered bales of about 75 lb, but a stationary baler could deliver over 100 cwt. The modern bales are up to half a ton in weight, and one man and a tractor can carry them home and stack them in the barns on his own, without having to leave his seat; it's no wonder he doesn't need the 5000 or so calories of fat bacon, porridge and suet pudding any more.

In 1953, we bought our first second-hand black-and-white television with a 9-inch screen, and being a newfangled thing, we had twenty-four people wanting to come and watch the Queen's coronation service on it. The morning came and the thing had three bands of revolving pictures for an hour before the service began, but righted itself as the viewers turned up. To see better, we drew the curtains from 10.30 a.m. until about 5.0 p.m. and everyone watched on in wonder, chomping on sandwiches and cakes all day. By the time the curtains went back, we were all sitting amidst a tip of papers, crumbs, spilt drinks, and you name it, but what a memorable day it was, and so marvellous to see it all on what was really no more than a modern radio.

We wanted to get rid of tuberculosis and abortion, we wanted to grow two blades of grass where only one grew before, and we wanted to carry more head of stock than our predecessors, even if we had to chop off the horns in order to get a large herd of peaceful cattle living together in harmony. The water was newly piped to the farm, and so we wanted hot water, too, and a bath tub to go with it. The dolly tub was too great a strain on Alice when she had the children to look after as well as the students adding to the housekeeping chores.

One thing that I dismally failed to do, because of a lack of money and a background of earth closets, left me with the most awful task of emptying the outside lavatory bucket. This awful contraption was referred to as an Elsan, but as it used to fill up daily, it saw no Elsan disinfectant! There was no point. But having to do that chore for about eight years, rather than digging out a proper sewage system, leaves me wondering today what was wrong with me at the time. Of course, there were no JCBs then, and our efforts were concentrated more on the work in hand, than on an inherited method of garden loo, but that much is history. The said bucket was like a magnet to each and every one of us, be it inhabitants or visitors, and I would be forced to empty the brimming, stinking bucket, a task which I detested and yet still accepted as a necessary evil. I wonder why I never thought to do anything about it.

Our students came from very diverse backgrounds, and they used to pick our still-immature brains for information, which kept us in a state of energetic euphoria, as we were all training for new world-breaking methods out of the old-world order of things, for a new way of facing the future. Gordon Bland was the son of a parson, who had worked in South America for many years as a missionary. He then took a parish in Herefordshire at £400 per year. Gordon was keen on photography and archery, and kept a Bible under his pillow. Later on, he went on to Northern Rhodesia poultry farming on a large ranch.

John Tyrrell's father was a consultant for Rolls-Royce, specialising in oils amongst other civil engineering areas. John left school, worked for a time in a Guest Keen and Nettlefold Factory, before becoming an officer in the army, where he was posted as an engineer to India, before studying agriculture for his chosen career. He married my sister Wyn and finished up farming a large area, and won an OBE for his service to agriculture. Under his pillow one would expect to find his pipe, which he cherished.

Wyn and Dad on her wedding day - 1951

When at the Whytehouse, our man Mick came to work on a Triumph Twin motorbike, which was rather a heavy machine when the roads were icy, and poor Mick had to be hauled from under it on several occasions. One day, he rang up to say the bike had died at Bewdley, wondering if I could tow him home. Anyway, we tied a wagon rope around the handlebars and set off, giving him a good space between us, but after a couple of miles I forgot all about poor Mick until he tooted us down, explaining that at about 70 mph, he was taking the corners like a slingshot and could we please cool it a bit. That old V8 really went when it wanted to. When towing John Adams' Austin to get it started, we asked him after the first half mile if it was going yet, to which he replied that he still hadn't even managed to get it into gear. I have to admit though, that we had gone through several gateways by that time, so I expect he was too busy steering to worry about changing the gears.

Another time, Mick's daughter June said she was by the police station at Rock, and wondered if I could give her a lift home, as it was late and getting dark. On the way home, she said that the policeman had been keeping her company until I had turned up, and as each car had approached, he was apparently saying, "Not this one, its too slow; not this one, the lights are too bright,' until I came over the hill and he said, "That's him". How daft we are when young and how knowledgeable and helpful the village bobby was then, too.

Another farmer near Stourbridge lived on a sewage farm taking waste from Brierley Hill and Dudley. As the Palethorpes' sausage factory was on the system and with pork being good carriers, his herd succumbed to foot and mouth disease on several occasions and he was thereafter forbidden to have any cloven-hoofed animals on his land again, so he reared horses instead. The soil was very sandy and well drained in that area, and was excellent for soaking up the run-off liquids.

His daughter Adeline was in fact my godmother. She had no family and decided to adopt a little girl, and when she and her husband went to collect the baby they were told that she was one of twins and they needed to be reared together. "That's fine, wrap them up and we'll go," said Adeline, but her stupefied husband said, "Here, wait a minute, let's discuss the matter – we only came for one." What else! Needless to say, the decision was made and the two children had a very good home and became a credit to them.

Another household we knew of was rather disorderly, and one had to fight to cross the room past all the furniture and what have you. They were a lovely loving family though, and were very proud of the inscription in 6-inch lettering over the fireplace, which read: 'Bless This Mess'.

Another student of ours was Mat Mathewson, the son of a maths wizard who was a bigwig in Indian educational work. I last heard that Mat was working on a farm in Rhodesia, before losing contact with him.

David Cullom came to us to try his hand at farming before his National Service stint, in which he spent his days mostly in Kenya at the time of the Kikuyu uprisings, and after meeting Alice's cousin Gladys when working with us, he went on to marry her, became a policeman and rose well through the ranks. His father, a major during WWII on the continent, became a tax inspector after the war.

Guido was a prisoner of war who was late in being released. He worked well and was a great man and a very capable countryman, who told me he slaved hardest of all for our team, especially me. He came from a good home in Germany, where he was a huntsman of bear and deer in the forests. I never heard from him after he left.

David Binnion was a student at Cirencester, studying forestry and estate management, who came to help us when on home leave. He was a big chap and we were in the midst of haymaking at the time, with thousands of hay bales to cart home. David worked his socks off and lost a stone in weight in the first week, but still came back for more whenever he was able. He became an auctioneer and an estate manager, eventually establishing his own arboretum near Kidderminster. He married a girl called Jennifer, who became a lady priest in those early years of change.

They were all first-raters, and it was in a way a sort of Kibbutz breakaway friendship.

As we have at last reached maturity in older age, I include some testaments to them: we will not be known as our League of Friends if I don't. Likewise included is an address I gave to the YFC fiftieth anniversary in 1992 in Kidderminster.

Years later, when we had started farming on our own, my father pitched up with eight cows he had purchased at a sale and said, "Here, lad, here's a start for you for working at home for eight years." We were forming a TT attested herd (tuberculin tested) and, unfortunately, these new cows were all reactors to the test, so it put us back another year in getting a licence! He had meant well and took the cows back, but could not quite comprehend the changes taking place and the modern approach to farming. It must be age, I suppose, as I also am confused over double-dutch talk of set-aside, quotas, subsidies, referendums, restrictions, animal passports, 30-month beef, veal calf export complications and EU interferences in all our laws, money and politics of today.

A Government Article in its Magazine

FROM BEEF TO MILK
Farming in the Rock Area
By
R. P. DONEY, N.D.A.

In these days of heavy capitalisation in farming, and when it is so difficult to get a start, it is interesting to record some of the achievements of a young farmer. Mr. John Butler entered Whitehouse Farm, Rock, in 1947. Total area is 164½ acres including 16 acres of waste land. The farm lies between the Old Red Sandstone belts of the Heightington basin and the Coal Measures area, so that some of the fields have a good depth of soil, whilst others quickly give way to brashy subsoils.

Most of the land is banky, typical of the area, which, in the past has been regarded as traditionally suited to rearing. Previous to Mr. Butler's entry this farm was devoted chiefly to beef, sheep, rearing and a little wheat.

Now Mr. Butler had been brought up on the light free working soils of the Clent area, with level fields and easy arable, and the change was therefore great. Having for a short time been connected with a herd of Ayrshires he decided to go in for dairy farming with this breed. Naturally the buildings were not suitable, so a shed was converted to a milking shed, with a dairy adjoining. The covered yard was retained and Parlour system adopted, and by careful planning the layout has been made very convenient and the conversions carried out at a minimum cost.

Much of the work of repairs to calf boxes and such like he did himself. Great care has been taken to make the buildings convenient for work, easy to clean yet as free from draught as possible and the sheds have been passed for T.T. milk production.

Mr. Butler has just constructed a cattle grid at the farm entrance with concrete and pipes and it appears to be working very efficiently, and can avoid the possibility of cattle straying, through callers forgetting to shut the gate.

CROPPING, ETC.

The change over to dairying called for a change in cropping, from wheat to beans, mixed corn, etc. The aim is to build up fertility, increasing humus through muck and leys to a standard capable of producing good crops of arable silage and grain followed by high-yielding leys.

The cropping is designed primarily for maintenance of dairy stock and about 5 acres of winter beans are planted to ensure adequate protein. In 1949 these were an excellent crop. In 1950 the layout was as follows—8 acres of wheat, 8 oats, 5 beans, 22 mixed corn,

4½ roots, and 15 oats and vetches to cut green for silage. Grazing and hay was provided by 25 acres leys and 57 acres permanent grass. This old turf consists of rough and banky fields which cannot be brought into rotation.

As much of the arable land as possible is autumn ploughed, and beans, wheat and some S.147 oats planted, and also the silage mixture of 100 lb. S.147 oats and 50 lb. vetches. When the silage crop has been cut it is ploughed up and the land planted again, partly with kale for winter carting, and the remainder with a mixture of rape and kale for eating off in the field. By this means the amount of roots, which are not easy to handle on this land, can be kept low.

The silage is made in a pit which holds approximately 250 tons, sited near the farm-yard, and has proved very successful.

Rotations have to be very fluid due to the variation of the fields, but the average is :—ley, wheat, beans, mixed corn, silage crop and kale, mixed corn (undersown).

The leys have so far been sown under nurse crops, and the mixtures varied from (1) perennial ryegrass-white clover, and (2) cocksfoot-white clover, and (3) ryegrass-cocksfoot-fimothy combined, plus some chickory and burnet in an endeavour to get a variation in grazing over as long a grazing period as possible. Any surplus can be cut for silage. Some of the leys sown after a couple of crops on what had previously been old turf may have to be renewed soon, as enough fertility has not yet been built up to enable them to last.

MANURING.

Soil analysis showed that all the fields were moderately acid, whilst the phosphate status varied from very low to moderate, and potash from very low to low. Lime has been applied to most of the land, and acidity will now be kept corrected by regular limings at 3 to 4 year intervals.

Grassland receives 6 cwt. per acre of compound manure annually and the crops a complete fertiliser above the normal rates to allow for the deficiencies, but the bean crop gets F.Y.M. at 12 to 15 tons per acre.

STOCKING.

The present stocking is much above the average for the area and Mr. Butler aims to increase his cattle still further from 34 cows to 40 with a corresponding increase of followers.

Soon after taking the farm he decided on Ayrshires and started with 19 heifers from Scotland and the breeding policy aims at a uniform herd of fine-boned, short legged cows with good formation capable of producing a 1,000 gall. average at 4% butter fat.

An attempt is being made to line breed to Bargower Blood. The present stock bull was by a proven sire out of a 1,800 gallon dam and the young bull was sired by Burnockstone Surpreme Title—a record priced bull which realised 5,800 guineas at the Bargower Sale 1948. This youngster has the appearance of making an excellent beast, and judging by his pedigree, should prove very valuable when used on the herd.

A few of the cows are pedigree and the remainder are being graded up.

The herd average for 1949/50 for 305 days was :—
  28 cows—823 gallons
  2 heifers—689 gallons

and the highest individual yield 1,864 gallons in 377 days, with butter fat of 5.06%.

Ginger, a cow of some 8 or 9 years has just gained 2nd place in the county trials for milk and butter fat and 2nd in the County Cup for yields with over 4.5% butter fat.

All the heifer calves are reared, being taken from the cow after the first day and fed by hand with 6 pints milk and 1 pint water for a fortnight. Gruel is then fed up to 14 weeks, after which they go on to a corn ration. Hay is introduced at an early stage and drinking water is always available.

Mr. Butler is a firm believer in S.19 for abortion and all young stock are vaccinated.

At 18 months heifers are fed hay and silage only. No cake is fed to cows in May, June and July and silage is used after Xmas.

SHEEP.

20-30 Clun breeding ewes are kept for crossing with a Hampshire ram for fat lamb production. The ewes are bought at autumn sales and sold out in late spring. Care is taken to keep the sheep well away from the milking cows.

A few poultry, usually about 200 are kept as a sideline, 80 of these being housed on the deep litter system which has been very satisfactory.

The management is based on the aim of self sufficiency, aiming at both a self contained herd fed as far as possible from the products of the farm, and returning the maximum manure to the land. A careful pursuance of this policy can only result in an increase in productivity beyond what is already at a very good standard.

The Unions, NFU, FWU etc., as now, did their best to support their members, but in their enthusiasm to outdo each other, they ran into the same trap as Scargill's miners. Complaining when things were tough was one thing, but to continually complain lost its sting, and when things got serious and were given vent to, farmers were jibed as, 'still moaning'. Were farmers only needed in wartime? Could the industry be allowed to decline? Need they be viable in times of peace, when imports were so cheap? Well, we found the answer when war broke out!

When war descended upon us, agriculture was at rock bottom, and with imported feed coming in at low prices, the British farmer, in order to survive, sacked his staff and practised dog and stick farming with his unpaid wife to assist him as needed. The 'once modern' machinery rusted in the sheds and the skills of the land depreciated with them.

The Depression had worn down this tough generation. Their arduous and thankless work had exhausted them. The challenge of the needs of war were too much, but now was the time for the young men, who had toiled for their fathers, but aimed to improve the situation for farming.

The Whytehouse days were sheer hard work and yet fun in their own way. It was a time of growing into adulthood and with others starting out into the wider world, it gave us all a glow. We had the cheek to believe our oyster was perhaps as the Beatles did – 'new, progressive, better' – and it was thus that youthful optimism evolved and drove us to continue into new territory.

African Voyage

Times moved on still more for us: we had always been churchgoers and our new vicar, Alex King at Rock, was a close friend and his family became one with ours. He had been in Africa doing missionary work and came to our parish to test his vocation in a different rural community and in a different line of work.

After a time, he tried to persuade us to go out and help in a foreign mission with whatever skills we could usefully adopt out there. What a hope – with a farm developing and now already upgraded; with a young family going to early school; with our own parents and kin to think of – it was quite out of the question.

"Well don't just dismiss it, go and see what happens elsewhere under your own church banner, just out of interest."

The next thing I knew was that I was approached by the Union Castle Steamship Company to escort a cargo load of pedigree livestock to South Africa, as cattleman in charge. I was to be given full command and responsibility, with my passage paid, all needs provided, and a wage into the bargain, which would cover my return.

This proved too interesting to refuse, so I joined the ship in London and we set off. My cargo consisted of a Guernsey bull, a dozen Jersey cows, some of which were in milk and all of which were in calf, several Longhorns, a number of sheep and a brood mare – Anne of Orange, in foal to Hyperion. This was a wonderful break and a pleasant passage was had, with full run of the ship, and to cap it all, the galley. As some milk was available from the cows, I did a deal with the cook; in exchange for my milk, I had first choice of the menus. Being a cargo boat, and ex-liberty ship of close on 20,000 tons, they carried about twelve passengers, as well as merchant cargo, so I was well off and in effect a first-class passenger. The hatches were lifted every second day for me to get at the rations for the livestock: hay, corn, bedding straw and a medicine chest. The manure was thrown overboard at sea, but not allowed in port, and could be a problem when it was allowed to pile up on deck, where it started to heat up and smell after a few days. In our wait for berths when we entered a harbour, so as to change our cargo, this meant that we could be up to a week at a time at each berthing, making the voyage from London to Durban a matter of six weeks or more.

Sketch of Cargo Boat Deck

The interesting thing I found on my voyage was that the animals, which were housed in pens on the deck, succumbed to seasickness. Even after being at sea for some time, they, with me included, remained sufferers of the inclement seas, and they soon became constipated. The only medicine I can recall using was Epsom salts (for them not me). My own remedy was to take to my bunk and hope to die.

One particularly nasty storm saw the side of the horse box caved in. Fortunately, is was a double box and the horse was secured on the furthest side from the storm, when a huge wave crashed down and smashed the other side, like a matchbox, even though built with 2-inch-thick timbers. Being in charge, I felt very important when forced to rush to the bridge and request that the Captain alter course, to enable the bosun and crew to wrap a cable round the pen and pull it up tight with a winch.

The first port of call was Dakar for fresh vegetable supplies. How we ever got them though was a mystery, because each time loading commenced, the stevedores all fell to their knees facing Mecca for a short break. The greens we took on board were all put into the ship's larder and then sprayed with potassium to sterilise them, which tasted horrible.

On another such trip we called in at Las Palmas for refuelling, and as it took five hours in the small hours of the night, we were able to go ashore. A lady passenger asked me to escort her for reasons of safety – ha ha – and what a safe trust it was, and we toured the shops. Even at 2.0 a.m., the shopkeepers opened up for us: "Don't need to buy, just look at our wares," which they lavishly displayed, opening up bales of materials, lace tablecloths, mementos of every description and, best of all, their wine. We were poured about six samples of various wines in quarter tumblers and then asked if we would like to purchase the bottles; needless to say, after somehow finding our way back aboard, we woke the next morning to terrible headaches.

The next port of call was called Lobito Bay, which was located behind a spit of peninsula that was aglow with colours from the hibiscus shrubs which lined it. It was the harbour for Luanda in Angola, and we unloaded forty tons of whisky and gin, which was to go inland to some thirsty customers in lonely, isolated hot spots in Namibia.

We also trans-shipped an Angus bull at Walvis Bay; as to what his future would hold, we could not imagine, as all we could see was miles of desert. Windhoek was the ultimate destination for the Angus bull and also for tons of barley for their noted beer from Walvis Bay. Windhoek, of course, was the capital town of a German colony in Namibia, which became a South-West African Protectorate after WWI, supervised from Cape Town.

My first experience of poor black servants was in loading herrings or pilchards by the ton. The heat was oppressive, especially in the bowels of the ship, and the Africans worked all day, half-naked, skin and bone, and slept on the streets until work all too soon began another day. We had had a little fracas on board with two Lithuanian seaman, who fell out with each other, resulting in one being half-killed by the other, who inflicted punishment on his head with a shoe brush. The pair were escorted ashore and tried by a magistrate, who had no clerk. Each and every word was repeated slowly and recorded, also very slowly, in long hand; this was memorable, because every second word was an unmentionable swear word and was hilarious to witness. They were duly separated and sent home on the next boat heading northwards.

Another interesting thing was the town, which had been built on desert and lacked shrubs, gardens or pavements. They had half an inch of rain a year, but were susceptible to flash flooding from a rare desert storm. The town consisted of the fish factory and its migrant workers, who had nowhere to go for relaxation. I entered the only pub, to find hordes of bodies strewn both inside and out, with shards of broken glasses littering the ground and the bar. I was informed that it was pay day, but reasonably peaceful by all accounts: "You should come on the fifteenth of the month, when they get their bonuses," they explained.

From there, we hit the Cape Rollers – unbroken, rolling waves, which caused the ship to slowly roll into the large troughs, shudder, and then slowly recover and go down the opposite side, so predictably as to make one retch for hour after monotonous hour.

Once we reached South African waters, our quarantine month began, and the animals had only a short time to recover before going onwards to their destinations. We were met in Cape Town by the farmers, who were importing this delivery of pedigree stock to improve their herds, flocks, etc., and there were lots of cameramen and reporters to welcome us. The opportunity was not lost to ensure one got invited to stay on their farms, and I and my family grew very close to a wonderful Afrikaner family from Davel, in the Transvaal, hundreds of miles up country. Mr and Mrs Grey's hospitality was exemplary, and our friendship lasted for many years. I recall them once explaining that they were unable to introduce me to all their relatives, as there was still resentment by many against the English from the times of the Boer War.

From there, I visited Rhodesia for a look-see; it was said that cars from all over the world were shipped, flat-packed, to East London, where, after assembly, they were driven up country. This provided a useful means of earning a free lift, by driving them to Bulawayo or Salisbury (now known as Harare). Driving over there was a mad and frightening experience, because where strip roads were in existence, one had to give up the right strip for any oncoming cars (seen or otherwise on ridges). As the sand between the strips wore quickly into deep gulleys and cars were driven at mad speeds, things got quite hairy. The only petrol available was often some 50 miles away, and, sometimes, only forty-five gallon barrels were served by a native at any hour, day or night, at the roadside. Strip roads can get very mobile after some hours and they can appear to swap sides in the shimmering heat haze, a bit like the UK skid signs.

The developed farms in Rhodesia were interesting; tobacco seemed a mainstay, but where irrigation was available, potatoes were grown and Scottish seed potatoes were imported in cardboard boxes in order to boost yields. Maize seemed to grow everywhere the land was less rocky, with varying crop successes. The poor cattle were reared on the ranch system, but required dipping, like our English sheep, to control ticks.

Having received my ship's pay, I started back homewards on the slowest airline possible. We took off in the morning, landed for lunch and passed the nights on land at various and varying digs. It was a wonderful way to get a glimpse of Africa. When we flew over Lake Victoria, we came in sight of a finger of land sticking out into the lake, and were told it was the airfield for Kampala. How on earth could we be expected to land on that tiny projection? Anyway, the pilot tipped the plane on its side and we dropped like a brick to near the water's edge and then landed across the peninsula, without even using the whole runway. Kampala was beautiful; a shower throughout the night and lovely fresh air made it my favourite to date, from the searing heat of the Sudan and Khartoum, to the riverboat on the Nile at Wadi Halfa. The desert was endless, with the occasional animal and perhaps the odd poor donkey, loaded down with huge panniers on either side, with its owner sitting precariously above its tail. We never discovered how they managed to find food in these regions – perhaps there was some mini oasis or other somewhere out there in the hot desert, which was like a lorry exhaust in your face, but I found it hard to believe this for even one moment.

The stopover at Malta was fascinating, and left an impression on me for life. There were home weaving looms, where beautiful weaving was contracted out; back gardens where crops of salads were shaded by vines and fruit trees, and rabbits ran amok, awaiting their turn in the stew pots; not forgetting the catacombs, where you walked down through the chalk passages. The sides of these passages were hollowed out for the corpses and then plastered in again; and then there was the domed church, where the German bomb went in through the roof amongst the congregation and never went off; and the palace tapestries from the fifteenth and sixteenth centuries, which lined the walls and were in need of some TLC to save them from disintegrating. Even the locals were nice, and they felt warmly towards the English, whom they regarded as friends, even though their leaders were jerking politics in a new direction since the war and having let the Russians into their naval dockyards in later years.

The last stop on the fourth day was at Nice for some lunch, which was very picturesque to look down on. But the greatest treat in store for us was as we came in low over Worthing to land at Heathrow. Having been away for so long and having previously been faced with burnt-up landscapes, we now had the privilege of seeing the English countryside in all its glory. The green fields, ripening corn fields, and green hedges were so beautiful, and it was worth leaving the country of my birth, so as to be treated to such a Garden of Eden on my return. Why was it that we never appreciated our own homeland when slaving between sixty and a hundred hours a week serving her?

The whole experience of arriving back home and settling down again was not so easy though after my travels, and each time I was asked to go and work in God's vineyards, it was all the more enticing, but not yet quite enough.

Then the final blow came – I was exposed to welding flash whilst repairing machinery, and my eyes had felt as though they were full of broken glass and my sight went. The doctor said I had only a fifty per cent chance of ever seeing again, and I remember the children kneeling between my knees, trembling and weeping. People even had to lead me to the toilet, leaving me feeling extremely vulnerable. It wasn't long before I rebelled against these kind offers of help and after three weeks, my sight gradually returned. You can imagine the relief I felt, and when I was next asked to go and serve the Lord, I was thankful to be able to say yes please. I could not fight God and win.

A move was put into place to sell up on a given Saturday auction and at 4.30 p.m., a phone call came out of the blue. It was the Union Castle Line asking if I could be at the docks at 5.0 a.m. the next morning in London, to take what was possibly the last exportation of livestock to South Africa. Is one's life always so preordained?

Alice was left holding the can; I caught the boat and did a one-way journey to our next destination through life. Alice paid our bills, sold or stored our possessions and took a flat with the children with friends, until it was possible to join me in Africa. How she managed to do so much on her own I will never know, but she did, which was made all the more creditable to her when her father forbade her to join me. She never saw him alive again, as he died before her return.

It must be said as to how brave Alice was through all this upheaval, because after I had dashed off on that last vessel as stockman-in-chief, Alice was left behind to pack up and sell, long lend, or otherwise dispose of our goods and chattels. After about six months and once the appropriate visas were in place, she set sail for Durban, South Africa, on a mail boat, which was fined in those days at a rate of £500 each hour that it was late with the post. My sluggish Drakensberg and Good Hope were slow, and took six weeks and more to get there, but the mail boats only took about, I believe, just under one and a half weeks to arrive at their destination.

As I waited on the quayside, there she was, with the three children, all full of life for the 'Big Adventure'. We had a couple of days to get their sea-legs sorted, and then it was off in a Morris Minor to cover the hundreds of miles distance along earth roads for our new home.

That poor little car was stretched and overloaded to the limits, both inside and out, as well as being loaded up on top, and our first stop was to be Kwa Magwaza, in Zululand, where we were to hang out for a short time, until our Portuguese 'residents' papers were authorised. On this particular mission, we stayed with Archdeacon Edward Arden, who at one time was the vicar of a church in Kidderminster near to the now Midlands Safari Park, which was then owned by Mr Harcourt Webb of Webb's Seeds. Ted, Betty, and daughter Mary were wonderful friends and still are.

On the way to Zululand, the roads became steadily worse and in places, we teetered down into the Dongas on stone surfaces, which was like riding on golf balls, and once committed, you could not stop; all you could do was hope to be able to climb back up on the other side. Daylight was closing in and the petrol gauge was showing nearly empty, which was another cause for concern. We had seen no sign of life for quite a while, let alone a petrol pump. At last, round a bend, we came across a Zulu man who was walking along the roadside and asked him the obvious questions. He said he would get in and take us to a store in the bush: even a cat would have had to be pushed into the Morris Minor, with all its trunks, cases and other paraphernalia, along with the five of us, but he made it and on we went. Eventually, he told us to leave the road and turn on to a bush track, which was where we eventually found the store. A guard with a shotgun had us covered and after a fracas, he let me go forth to a lighted house in amongst the trees. Imagine my surprise when the top half of a stable door opened and I was looking down the wrong end of a revolver at a nervous man's silhouette.

What sort of introduction was this for Alice? However, all turned out well and our hosts turned out to be emigrants from Devon, and they not only took us in, but fed us, bedded us, and led us many miles the next day through the Nkandla Forest to Kwa Magwaza, near to Melmoth.

Our hosts, the Ardens, thought we were lost being twelve hours late in arriving, but all was well and we were eternally grateful to find ourselves safe and well after a rather frightening adventure.

Maciene Drive

Our House at Maciene

Alice, Michael, Rozanne, Robert & John

Ploughing with Oxen

Cutting Down Reeds to Make a Carpet

Women Soiling over the Carpet

Schoolboys Planting Rice

Alice in Paddyfield

Schoolboys Harvesting

Monies donated by Oxfam were used to make the floating rice field as shown in the pictures above.

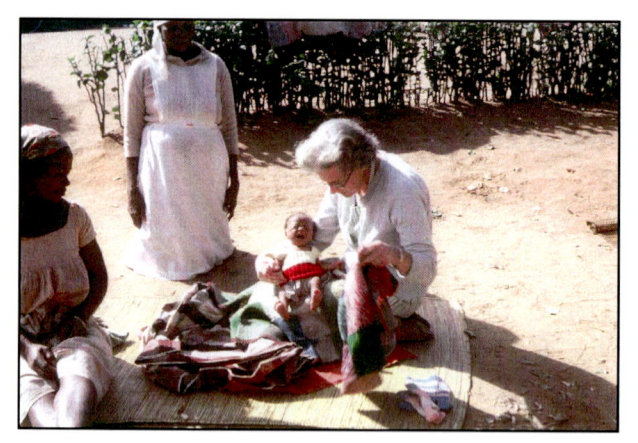

Alice at Mission Hospital

Maciene School

Maciene School

Girls Sewing

Re-roofing the cathedral

Outstation Church

Church Conversion

Blaenplwyf farm

Our Four

Generations

Wirral
Selattyn
Bryngolau Farm,
Llandysul
Blaenplwyf Farm,
Verwig
Cardiff

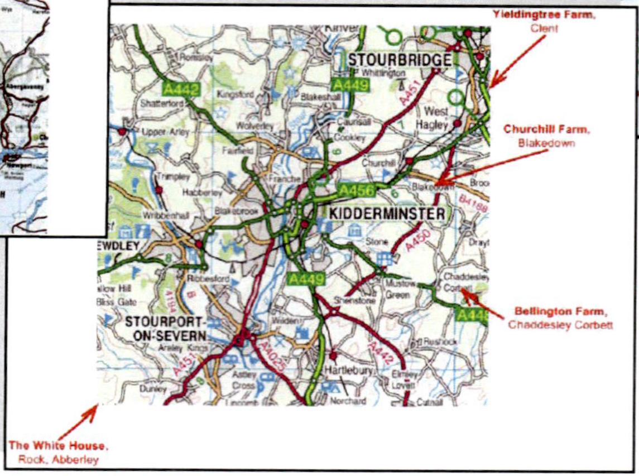

Yieldingtree Farm,
Clent
Churchill Farm,
Blakedown
Bellington Farm,
Chaddesley Corbett
The White House,
Rock, Abberley
STOURBRIDGE
KIDDERMINSTER
STOURPORT-ON-SEVERN

Msumba
Maciene
Pretoria
– Rozanno school
Johannesburg
– Michael & Robert school

Maciene

In due time, we were cleared for the off again and found ourselves once more sardined into our little car, as we headed out for Swaziland and Mozambique, and then the last 150 miles to Maciene. What a journey! To think that a girl from the town of Clitheroe, who was not allowed to switch on the radio when 16 years old in case she broke it, should be faced with such an ordeal with her children, in so foreign a land, where even her own tongue was not used, except in the house, and amongst so many strangers with alien ways and isolated into the bargain from her own kind, was very daunting indeed. Full credit was due to Alice in the way in which she adapted, blended, coped and, eventually, learned to trust and love these Shangaan people. They, in their turn, accepted us in the same spirit and the local African chief even requested that our Bridget, who was born amongst them on 21 December 1964, should be included as a member of the tribe, and that the name Macie (the Shangaan tribal name) be included in hers.

The Christmas service in church that year was packed, but imagine our amazement when we emerged to find ourselves surrounded by the Portuguese army, with rifles and machine guns at the ready. They suspected us of insurrection; anyway, after proving our innocence, we finished up with the army officers and administrator standing round Alice's bed drinking a 'whisky Merry Christmas' to mother and baby lying in her arms; what a contrast!

When Alice joined me, we spent several weeks in Zululand and Swaziland, and this was a great experience for us all. The Zulu singing and harmony is renowned and the Mothers' Union, which Alice joined, used to turn up in their self-imposed uniform of white blouses, black headdresses and skirts, which I believe was adopted to mimic the clergy vestments. As they were of the older generation, they were inclined to be of a fuller figure (traditional build), and we used to joke that they were weighed in as part of the inaugural ceremony.

When I reached Durban on my final voyage, a letter was waiting for me inviting me to go to Lourenco Marques in Portuguese East Africa, Mozambique. The Anglican mission had been built on agricultural concession land eighty years ago, and the land was not currently being farmed and, due to political stress, could be withdrawn. This act in itself could potentially lose the whole structure of the mission: the cathedral of the Lebombo diocese, the hospital, where 45,000 patients a year were being treated, the schools where 800 children were receiving an education (in the Portuguese tongue), and where all the administration buildings and European staff houses were situated, covering an area with forty outstation bush churches, as well as schools.

The farmland occupied two hundred acres and it would be my job to farm it and to possibly prevent a terrible catastrophe from happening. What a challenge! Was this what I had been schooled for? Why me? How to go about it? I was not a linguist by any means, and the official language was Portuguese, although those without an education only knew their native tongue, which was based on the Zulu tongue, but had over six variations through Swazi and Shangaan, up to the Tanzanian borders. It was also at a time that was only 60 years after the events depicted in the film *Zulu*, where Chinyanga met up with the more common Northern Swahili.

Firstly, the soil consisted of two hundred acres of what could only be described as sand-dune quality, and no markets or labourers were available to me at the time. In the fertile valley of the Limpopo River, the crops were fruitful and of good quality, but this land had been farmed using the traditional way of clearing, taking two crops and then reverting again for recovery for a season over a number of years. The first answer was to build a boarding school for boys, who lived too far away to get even the most basic of educations. They could then get free boarding and schooling by working in the fields each afternoon in lieu, thereby doing three things to help the process with which I was now tasked: getting an education, providing labour for the farm and also giving an outlet for the crops that had been produced.

We even managed to procure a herd of suckler cattle and a Brahmin bull, which could be used by the local herds to improve the quality of the cattle in the area. These cattle were herded into the bush and corralled each night. The bulls were used for plough oxen, the manure as fertiliser, and they had to be dipped each week, because of the ticks which, in turn, caused East Coast Fever; this task in itself entailed a walk to the cattle-dip 5 miles away.

The maize crops were not of the best quality, but sufficient for our needs. We grew rice on the edge of our nearby lake, and onions and tomatoes were grown out of season on that same land. Peanuts were greatly called for and these produced well. Sweet potatoes were another form of crop, as were our coconuts and oranges, when we managed to get them producing, that is. Cotton and castor oil did not do so well though and so we discontinued growing those after a while. Some special grasses were also introduced and these grew well, but were not made much of, due to the heavy labour requirements of hand planting and the hauling of it to the cows.

Milk was out of the question; the high humidity and poor grazing were against us there and the calves needed all that was available to them. It was only rarely that I saw milk being taken from a cow and to see the milker spitting on his hands both to get the milk flowing and to keep going, it was not an encouraging sight.

The bulls were castrated at nearly two years of age, when they would be broken to the plough for about five years. With a year out to rest, these were then sold on for prime beef. I was horrified when I saw the local castrator at work, using a stake and a lump hammer to perform the operation, but it was effective and consisted of pulling the testicles over the stake and crushing the cords with the hammer in much the same way as the famous Burditzo pliers were used in Europe.

During a drought year, 'War on Want' sent some money to help the starving people and I was given the job of distributing maize flour. In the outstations, it was our clergymen who selected the most deserving, but the local tribes were treated differently.

Our own rice fields were situated around the edge of the lake and were about 20 yards wide. Whenever we had heavy rains they flooded and in drier times, they dried out and failed, so we cut down the bulrushes and reeds and made a carpet over the root systems. A layer of soil was then carried over from the drier sides and a field of three to four inch soil depth was formed over this matting, to become a floating rice field. This way, no matter whether we had drought or flood, we were assured of good rice crops. The workers for this task were paid in maize meal, in the process fulfilling the Chinese proverb, which says, 'it is better to give a starving man a fishing rod than a fish', so we did both, and it was gratifying to hear the method was being used later in other wet areas by the native Africans.

Maciene Farm

Farm planting and harvesting has continued normally, the latest venture being the planting of 200 coconuts, half as seed and half as plants. We hope that we shall be able to rear to maturity at least 60% of these during the next eight years. Other crops doing well are beans, rice, sweet-potatoes, mealies and the banana trees planted only a short while ago are already producing fruit.

One of our troubles is that the tractor is completely worn out and each time we try to use it something breaks or cease to function, and the cost of repairs are more than the value of the machine. Another trouble is the lack of fertility. When funds are available we hope to be able to keep and rear cattle. This venture would not only provide us with manure for fertilising the ground, but also fresh milk and, at times, meat.

(Extract from article by Mr. Butler)

Note. – There have been many enquiries about the farm lately and readers of the *Lebombo Leaves* may like to know that the farming of our land at Maciene is vital. Not only does it provide food for the enormous number of mouths we have to feed but it also, by virtue of it being cultivated, fulfils the conditions by which we were granted the whole plot of land together with the Mission established on it. – Ed. 1960

Having established the principles of using the land, we turned our attentions to other needy projects. Small churches in the bush were built in the traditional fashion, with reed walls plastered with wet sand and cow manure. Each would have a thatched roof and a floor made from cow dung, laid in the same way as cement, which would be polished when set. Over the years, we started replacing several of these churches using block walling and corrugated roofing: the congregations saved up for the materials and carried water to the sites, and our job was to train up a team of builders, carpenters, plumbers, etc. and do all the work.

Africans are used to building round houses, and we had to teach them to build in straight lines. We had no stone, so we bought cement and made our own bricks with a compressed sand/cement block maker; the blocks were watered daily for a month to mature. A skilled man taught others in each department, so that we could take on whatever was thrown at us. We drew up our plans, bought most of the raw materials and then could construct a house, hospital, school or church, complete with plumbing and electric wiring where necessary, making the furniture, doors and windows where needed. We even serviced the vehicles ourselves and eventually, when someone left to go to the city and earn good money, we felt we had contributed to a worthwhile cause.

Some of our successes proved very stressful to us as amateurs, including the digging of a substantial well, where we could pump 3,000 gallons of filtered water per day, and the building of a water tower in order to get pressure through the taps.

As the school grew in size and with increasing numbers visiting the hospital, it became essential to build a toilet block; this sounds simple, but was a challenge to us, as no one used toilet paper; instead, they used maize cob middles, stones or anything else available to them, and this in turn blocked the drains. Large volumes of water were needed to flush the toilets, which we did not have and could not afford, and a large soakaway was also needed for its disposal. We solved this by building cubicles above a large septic tank. Each squat had 3-inch outlets and straight 4-inch pipes were submerged in the water, thus forming a non-blockable basin, with a smell trap below. The soakaway was not hard-pressed, and the only water required to keep the whole system sweet was about six buckets of water each evening for it to be able to cope with possibly 2,000 callers or more. This, I am told, is still in use after forty-five years.

We also planted coconuts in the fields, but these were dug up and eaten. Those which survived this hazard had a funny way of walking into other peoples' patches when about 2 feet high, so, to resolve this, we ended up planting them in the garden and planting out as they grew larger. Bananas were grown without a problem, and in our own garden we had many fruits which needed early help with water and nurture, before being planted out. We had avocado, pawpaw, orange, lemon, naartjie, bananas, vines, granadillas, mango and mulberry, etc., but these were not used for large-scale production.

The singing of the Shangaans was not as musical as that of the Zulus, but they were excellent harmonisers and loved to produce a play at Christmas and Easter. We also had a printing press, which, although old, was a heavy cast-iron set of machines. These originally came from the UK by ship, and were lowered into the bay at Inhambane and retrieved at low tide. They were then transported the last 160 miles by lorry. Americo was our trained printer (with an assistant), and we produced prayer books, Catechisms, New Testaments, hymn books, etc. in about eight languages. The lead letters would be fitted into the moulds and then pressed on to a flat surface and printed for editing, before running them off on the treadle presses. The books would then be trimmed by the guillotine and were put into Alice's book shop, where they were sold for the odd Escudo and were valued all the more for having been paid for, rather than if they had been gifted. It is human nature to value something which is expensive, as opposed to if it just appears in with the junk mail.

Our weekly shopping was a tedious part of the week. We needed diesel oil for the generator and water pump, oil, paint, nails, timber, glue, etc. for the carpenter and painter, cement and reinforcing, etc. for the builders and all the refinements we could afford. We also needed wine, candles and brooms, etc. for the church, food for the seminarians, meat and dried fish for the boarding school, and buckets, mops, candles, and whatever else was required for the hospital.

We then started purchasing things for the workers, staff, nurses and visitors, coupled with the collection of the mail from PO Box 63, and any other shopping for anyone who supplied us with a list and some money. In that humid heat, this task was a marathon in itself, but just imagine the task of distributing and accounting for it all at the other end, not to mention the change that had to be returned when one arrived back home. Alice was involved in this expedition for thirteen years, even though she was an unpaid appendage and the only married white woman in the diocese; she served as an anchor for all and sundry, she was the diocesan hostess, and she catered for all visitors from far and wide. She helped with the storerooms and seminary, the MU work, and the St Agnes Girls Guild, as well as working in the bookshop, performing the weekly shopping and postal collections, counselling the aggrieved, and often being called out to kill the odd snake which caused such a panic. When we had synods, the clergy from far and wide congregated and we had the pleasure of the company of the Archbishop of Cape Town and also the

Archbishop of Central Africa as our guests, not to mention another dozen bishops, archdeacons, senators, ambassadors and consuls at various times; add to these maybe twenty or so African priests and various other helpers, and they were all catered for and their digs found by Alice.

The aim of mission work was threefold – care of the body with food and health care – care of the mind and education – and care of the soul with Church and teaching.

Going back to Maciene; during this influx, our helpers would meet relatives they hadn't seen for some time and we suffered the consequences from the indigenous staff over-imbibing with them late into the night. Imagine the indignation Alice showed when Mateus, our house servant, cleaned the bath with salt and the meal was splashed with Vim. Fried Salad! Having added Vim to the soup, he ate the mangos and the stones were served up to our guests. On another memorable occasion, twenty eggs were put in to boil in a dry saucepan, and a further incident saw the meal being late when someone forgot to light the cooker and so on. Scraped, charred toast was also not forgotten at such special times.

One of the problems of the mission was caused by the isolation, the humidity, the absolute draining of the body and soul by the remoteness and the continual giving out of oneself and being unable to unload, or share the problems of the work with anyone. This eventually, as seen in so many cases, led to a necessary sundowner now and again, and ultimately breakdown by a large percentage of the saints of missionaries, who gave their all for the cause. The very size of the 'vineyard' beggared belief, and the workers seemed so few. Maciene alone had about forty-six outstations covering say five thousand square miles, and this was run by a handful of Africans and one European priest; the tracks to so many were sandy and remote, reached only by foot, bicycle or hitch. The schools were few, being so far out, and consisted of different children for the afternoon sessions, and were built with reeds and thatch, or were even under the trees. Catechists were used for lots of these places and they also led matins in the churches and prepared others for confirmation. We served the church in our own different callings and have a common bond and many joint memories.

Amusing occasions cropped up and one such occasion was with Alice, when on one of her greater-than-usual shopping sprees, such as when we went to meet the children from the Lourenco Marques trains for holidays. She became friendly with the wife of a large store in Lourenco Marques, who was Chinese, and they discussed all wifely matters, particularly the Chinese lady's mother-in-law problems. They knew no common language such as Portuguese, but with Alice in her English tongue and her friend in Mandarin, they still managed to get on fine. I never really understood how they both managed to communicate and I thought it rude to even enquire.

Whenever we were in Lourenco Marques, our treat was a Chinese meal in town in the evening, with chicken piri-piri being a must. When you ordered, you'd wait for the bird's squawk, and then when it arrived on huge plates and was so highly spiced, it made you wonder how it was possible to eat so much. After a struggle to clear the plate, we were then brought the other half. In the humidity and with collar and tie and starters of king prawns, it was always a memorable occasion and took a long time to get through. Only when the chairs were being stacked on tables for sweeping up at 2.0 a.m., did one realise what a mammoth task it all was. Unfortunately, we could only manage these so-called mini-breaks about three or four times a year, but what a release it was when we did.

Our friend Mr Gedge was a very pedantic ex-civil servant, who had once been on Foreign Service with the consulate office in Brazil. He was so set in his ways that we took the mickey behind his back, even though he was (or because he was) such a mainstay as the diocesan secretary. We enjoyed his company immensely; he would take us out to dine whenever he could and he was a real gourmet – even his wines were impressive. First he read the label, then took the temperature, then tasted the wine, before we even got a look in. Then he would drink a silent toast to Bonny Prince Charlie to the enchanting wave of the glass: up, across, round and then the sup. He even had a special ruler cut to exactly 4 inches for the signing of cheques; if anyone was so much as an Escudo out in the accounts, the correspondence would continue by post (costing money in stamps), until everything balanced out correctly.

He enjoyed a G&T for his sundowner and on one occasion, when off for home leave, he told the bishop that if he did not return for whatever reason, the crate of gin in his room was for him. He was travelling light with a number of empty suit cases at the time, so as to restock his wardrobe whilst away. The bishop said that he listened to every newsflash, but there was no crash, so he lost out on the possible chance of a gin cache. The poor man retired and was later buried at Maciene Cemetery – he was held in the highest esteem by everybody.

Maciene

Another old faithful was Eva Gibson, who spent over fifty years at Maxixe in Mozambique, walking miles per day, often without shoes on her feet, teaching and guiding in those far off days, with true missionary zeal, until she eventually expired. She was a true friend of the family and was a source of much inspiration from her example and courage.

Eventually, a young priest, Harry Leak, helped her and took over the work after her demise. He was a valued friend and a linguist of renown, who took communion service in about twelve different languages as well as in Morse code. Forty years later, he still pays an occasional visit to us on his old motor bike and will always be more than welcome.

Inhambane was a trading post of long ago and slaves were captured and held there for shipment in the dhows to the Zanzibar slave markets. The rings are still in the walls to this day, to which they were manacled in those sad days all those years ago. The bay is encircled by coconut and mangrove trees and is very attractive. To cross over to Maxixe was an experience in itself. The ferry boats were all owned and run by the local population, who were of African and Indian descent, and carried ten or fifteen passengers with sacks of purchases, poultry tied by the legs, or produce: tangerines, naartjies, coconuts, mandioc, maize, sweet potatoes, or what have you. As there was no pier, it meant a short knee-deep paddle to get aboard. The ladies were carried by two men sitting upon their crossed arms, but the men were carried on the shoulders. It was a real treat to see a stranger being chased along the shore with a man's head between his legs when his decorum said it would be preferable to get his own legs wet. These boats could be hired to sail the bay and for very little money, but a picnic on a sunken wreck and a lazy rocking trip through the hot hours of the day provided a welcome relief. The single tricorn sail was never taken down and with a flick of the jib, away you went.

A hunter once gave Father Wright a quarter of a joint of venison and as he had no fridge to store it in, he marinaded it every day. On one particular visit to Maciene two weeks later, he gave us a piece, which was still sweet, juicy and fresh, which we thought was magic, albeit asking for food poisoning. There was also a sort of fish much like plaice, which was caught off the shoreline and called moonfish. It was delicious, but the dried fish and crabs we bought for the boarding school contained small crabs and shark fins, and the boys would not eat shark meat, as sharks were man eaters like the crocodiles, and one did not eat the spirits of one's ancestors.

Charles Wright was a very experienced priest, who had taught at one of England's top private schools before taking Holy Orders. However, he was somewhat 'over the heads' of many mission scholars. One day, Bishop Stanley invited him to give a lecture to the seminary students at Maciene and the bishop later quizzed the class as to how they had enjoyed the lecture. Their reply was, "Very much, my Lord, but please could you explain what he was talking about."

Another time when Charles was priest in charge at Maxixe, a schoolmaster left at short notice and Father Wright took the class himself for a period, until a replacement was found. One of his sessions of maths was rather confusing to the pupils. You see, they were told that it was 370 miles to Lourenco Marques, and his Land Rover did 25 mpg, so how much would it cost to get there at X-amount of escudos per litre? As this seemed a bit over their heads, he simplified the question by saying, "No, tell me instead how many dead cats would be needed to line the route if they measured 20 inches each." The class was absolutely floored, as they could not even begin to visualise catching so many cats from the area, it would take weeks! He gave up shortly after and found another teacher!

Before our time out there, a priest had taken a group of thirty children across country to the beach of the nearby Indian Ocean, where they enjoyed themselves for a time, but on the way back, a head count revealed six boys missing. Every eighth wave was larger than the rest and when it crashed down on the steeply shelving shore, it had a powerful undertow, which is where the boys were believed to have disappeared. Years later, we saw many strangers all heading in that direction with pots, pans and sleeping mats, and so we asked them what was going on. It appeared that one of the boys of twenty years ago that had been lost in the tragedy had walked out of the waves some miles away and announced that they would all appear on the beach where the tragedy had happened on the next full moon, and these relatives were going to spend the night on the shore calling them out. None did, but one was seen in the half light for a short on-off spell!

When we were invited to some of the weddings we were given honoured seats at the top tables under palm sunshades, where we were made most welcome. We realised how chosen we were when around us, inside a stockade, were the wider members of the family, cousins and friends, and outside the stockade were the neighbours and acquaintances, who were not allowed in, but were welcomed to the party even so – the meals and the drinks were the same for us all though. Those on the top table had wine and beer, but for the others, a brew had been especially prepared from fermented maize flour, which looked milky and was very potent. In the cashew season, the nuts were sold for petty cash, but a sort of apple on which the nut grew was fermented, as we do with cider, and then distilled in illegal stills, and it was so potent that syphilis spread rapidly as a result.

Guests of Honour & God Parents too in the course of time

In due course, babies came along, and we became godparents to quite a few of them. It took years to realise just how much we were befriended. One day, someone came and said he would be away for a few days at a wedding sixty miles away. As there was no transport and the venue could only be reached along trails in the sandy bush, I enquired as to how he intended getting there.

"Oh," he said, "by bike."
"But you haven't got a bike."
"No, but Ernest has," he replied.
"But what if Ernest says no?"
"Oh, he can't," said Philimao, "he's my friend."

It was then that I realised why I had so often felt taken for granted in doing small tasks, taxiing, etc. for them. I was accepted as a friend, and therefore I must serve them as they were prepared to serve me/us in any way we needed them.

One day, a duiker (the smallest of antelope) was brought to us as it had been by its mothers side when she had been shot. It had several perforations in its ears and as it was too young to eat, we reared it and became its adoptive parents. 'Sunny' was reared in the house and garden with the other pets, and shared everything with all of us, even leaping on the settee and having the run of the garden. Sunny could not stand black people, and it was not unknown to hear cries for mercy and help coming from the trees where he had driven them for safety. He was a real character and would go round all the ashtrays eating the cigarette butts, and would imbibe any glass of beer an unwary guest had put down.

Sunny our Duiker pet who shared the house with our pets

Eventually, as we were going on leave for six months, we donated him to the zoo in LM, where he was safe and secure; whenever we could, we called to see him, and he always came running and remembered us all. A cigarette and beer was not forgotten, either; he was a family member in his own right.

Robert, at about 4 or 5 years of age, purchased a pig from Father Josias, who was a lovely old priest in his eighties. He had chosen the runt of the litter, as it had dear little sticky-up ears. Well, Little Pig Robinson grew and grew, and it coincided with a time when the hens were disappearing in the night. It would be unlikely to be a thief and must have been a wild ferret or such, so we lay in wait with a torch. When a hen squawked at about 1.0 a.m., we dashed out and caught the culprit red-handed. It was Piggy, who had found he could now reach up high enough to pull the hens from their perches and have an enjoyable midnight snack.

We were also given a sheep called Oswald, which took to Robert and followed him everywhere. At mealtimes, it insisted on standing under the table with its nose breathing on his knee, and if shut outdoors, the noise was intolerable. It went on like this until one day it got a cord wrapped round one if its legs. It tightened enough to act as a tourniquet and the leg went gangrenous. But the tame monkey we were glad to get rid of; it was smelly and seemed to get the runs whatever the diet. Never again will we contemplate having another.

Our new cook, Sina, was a wonderful woman; an English-speaking Zulu and the daughter of a Presbyterian minister. She had met her Shangaan man whilst he was working a stint on the mines in Joburg, married him and came to his Maciene home only to find he already had another wife. What ensued I am not sure, but as she was better educated and perhaps for other reasons, she became wife number one. Her bed was an enormous Victorian mahogany monster with drawers built into it. I asked her where she'd got it from and, apparently, it transpired that it had come from Joburg. "How did you get it home?" I asked. "We posted it!" Whenever the children came home for the holidays, she would get out her Mrs Beeton and find something special for them; she always cooked to a turn. Her son was called up to fight in the war and we discussed the future for him afterwards. She said she had a phobia about the 'rebels' in the north sending him to Libya or Russia for officer training, as he was doing so well at school; he might then marry a white girl.

Apartheid did not exist in Mozambique other than a natural partition, and an educated black man had a vote, whereas a Portuguese woman did not, unless she had a degree. Sina said she did not like to mix the different backgrounds, as, separately, they had a complete life in their own social standing, but as hybrids, they belonged nowhere. They themselves could be happy, but the children paid a price! "Mixed marriages – no way," she said. She is still alive and reading without glasses, despite the fact that she must be about eighty now, content in her surroundings and cared for by her family. A lovely, lovely lady.

The boys were cricket mad and Robert was constantly trying to outdo our fast bowlers; so much so that the boarding school at White River felt it necessary to inform us beforehand of a charge to be added to the next school bill, as it would contain an extra charge for thirty new panes of glass. We assumed he was overzealous. Their headmaster had been a Japanese prisoner of war and was a tremendous man, who was admired by everyone. Whether it was joy or sorrow, Robert used to trade money for punishment for his friends, but on being found out, he said that the extra thrashing meted out made the practice unviable. Events were interesting: at home they folded the hens' heads under the wings and rocked them gently for a few minutes and they went to sleep lined up in a row. On the trains they carried snakes to and from school and caused panic to the passengers. During the school breaks they went home with their friends and recounted some of the exploits, and told of what fun they had – balancing a bucket of urine against a front door and knocking, before beating a hasty retreat, and watching from cover as the door opened and the hall got a drenching being only a part of it. Or watching someone stamping out a burning newspaper on their doorstep, containing dog mess wrapped carefully inside it. Not our boys, of course!

When we flew home on a TAP Portuguese plane for the last time via LM, Beira, Luanda, and Portugal, we were given a small bottle of wine each with our meal, which we asked to be changed from Dao for Seradya. We were brought the other wine, but we were also left with the originals, and the resultant array of bottles on our trays was impressive. The Lusitanian bishop, Bishop Pereira, was travelling with us and moved many of these bottles on to his tray, too; as he put it, 'to share the shame'. How gracious!

We never saw a bull fight, but the Portuguese always took pride in not killing their bulls, just a little salve on the wounds to heal them up, rather than the Spanish method of ending the affray.

The mealies (sweetcorn) in the Limpopo valleys, grew well and were much better than our own sandy fields could hope to produce. The native system of farming by growing two crops and fallowing for two or three years saved bleaching or ruining the habitat.

In order to get more water each day from our lake, we had to increase the size of the well. We dug a circular trench with the bottom slanting down on the outer edge, that was a foot (12 inches) wide, with a 13-foot diameter; this, we filled with reinforced concrete. Then we dug out both the centre and beneath the walls of this circle, so that the entire thing sank into the sand, the outer edge end now chiselled its way down. The sides were left unbound, because as we kept building it up with 9-inch blocks, the leading edge was always wider. It was located on the edge of our rice field lake, so that the lake water percolated the sand for 160 feet in order to purify it, before it entered the base of our new well. We dug and built as fast as possible, until the incoming water was faster than our baling crew could keep up. We pumped each morning, so that the water could settle for twenty hours and rid itself of impurities in suspension. The pump was driven by an old diesel engine, which used to drive the generator, hence its twin flywheels (needed to stop fluctuations in flickering lights).

The storage tank was a headache though, as we needed to get height in order to gain water pressure in the taps and it also had to be built on light sand, with a mushroom-top tank. It had to be strong enough to withstand one hundred tons balanced on top of it without cracking or tipping, and without an engineer to advise us, it meant several sleepless nights. We dug the foundations where no stone, clay or anything hard existed; we watered and compacted the base, and then we built a round tower, which was supported with a square inside it in home-made compressed blocks. When we reached our desired tank height, we formed a convex base reinforced with rods similar to the effect of a bicycle wheel. The spokes were then bent upwards at the circumference and built up either side with water-resistant filling, hoping it would be waterproof and strong enough not to telescope down the stem when subjected to a large load. It did not – and is still in use forty years later.

Late one night a goat was heard crying out in distress about a quarter mile away. There was a thicket where some heathens had lived for years and we had moved them away, it being on mission land. Even in daylight it had a sort of haunted, eerie feeling, and in the centre were the remains of abandoned kraals. Trees surrounded the deserted area and skulls of animals were nailed to them, whitened with age, but it was creepy nevertheless. Anyway, this goat cried and cried and in the end, I had to go out in the early hours to try and help it. I walked around the area and pinpointed the spot, but, in the pitch darkness, could not find a way to it, so went to the furthest point which had an entrance path to the centre. Groping along this path, I came to the *kraal* precincts and in stepping over the boundary entrance, my hair suddenly stood on end, my face froze and I felt bewitched and almost paralysed. In an unusual desperate rush, I reached the opposite side of the enclosure and as I stepped out on to the path again, my hair dropped back down, my face felt warm again and the goat had silenced and disappeared. I am not a brave man, and this experience left me very conscious of another spirit world, which I found terrifying to experience contact with. I could have turned back to find out more, but only if I was mad or going that way. I didn't.

For us, it was comforting to have the hospital nearby in case of an emergency. One night, when Robert had malaria, a nurse sat with him all night, reading aloud to keep him awake, as his temperature was about 106 degrees and he said pink elephants were climbing the walls. The fever, thank goodness, broke by about 5.0 a.m. and he recovered. Malaria was a common problem and if it was cerebral, it could even cause death. From its onset to death, it could take as little as two hours, which did not give enough time to enable one to get treatment.

One of the nasty diseases was bilharzia, which was caused by the legs being punctured by mites in watering places, where one might be crossing or washing in the shallow lakeside. The parasites followed the blood vessels, growing into maggots, and migrated to the stomach and liver, resulting in the need for seventeen injections into the stomach wall by way of treatment over the course of seventeen days. Rabies was similarly treated, and the patient went mad if not treated in time. Alice was scared of such an attack and the implications of what this could mean to the family. Mango fly could get under the skin's surface and maggots kept forming from the sac it produced; each time, they laid more eggs before being squeezed out, so were hard to eradicate.

As the hospital was always short of modern medicines, the doctor used alternative treatments where possible. On one occasion, I suffered from heat rash on my head and was told to rub used sump oil well in each night, as the sulphur in the used oil would put it right. Well, it may very well have done, but Alice put her foot down and said I was not sleeping on her linen like that, and who did I expect to do the laundry afterwards?

The laundry was an interesting task: clothes were washed and then threshed over concrete drainers, and then ironed with heavy charcoal irons, which were swung overhead to get the charcoal glowing and to up the heat.

Our hot-water systems were large 45-gallon oil drums sitting on a steel grill and bricked in to preserve heat. Wood was fired from below and was very effective, as the hot water could then be piped into our baths or showers. Eventually, we had all European houses fitted with flush toilets and septic tanks, hot water and fridges.

Water was a general problem. We Europeans stored our rainwater from the roofs in large underground tanks and boiled it before use. The Africans had to live away from water, because of the malarial (anopheles) mosquitoes, and had to walk great distances every day to get water for their own use, be it four miles or more away. The women were given this division of chores, and one often saw women plodding home, with 4-gallon tins of water on their heads (40 lb), sticks for the fire or food in each hand, with a baby tied to their backs in the traditional *coplana*. We were obviously thirsty in the heat of the day and if they saw us, they would offer us a drink from their hard-earned supplies. But as it was not boiled, we had to diplomatically decline, although we were always impressed by their generosity. Africans are very clean people and at every opportunity, they will wash hands, face and legs; before a meal, they will use some of that hard-earned water to rinse their hands.

At one time, the government installed wells and pumps for health reasons, but they soon broke down and resulted in everyone lowering containers into the deep, leaving a contaminating scum behind for everyone else. We used a well for the mission and pumped about 3,000 gallons daily into our brick reservoirs, but we had to keep all taps locked, because of the cost of our precious resource and because of the risk of contamination. Whenever a gang collected to draw water, it became a boggy mess from washing and wastage.

When the new main road was tarred, the traffic flow was much faster and this was not at first appreciated by the women, who carried long bamboo sticks on their heads. As you neared them at speed, they would turn slowly around to see what was approaching, leaving you with the only option being to either stop or speed up, before the sixteen-foot sticks blocked the road. It was a bit like a railway crossing barrier coming down in slow motion, but without the flashing lights forewarning you.

Before tar was introduced, the sandy roads used to rut badly from the wheels of vehicles, and brakeless cycles descending into a valley had no way of stopping or changing direction, so they used to go head-on into each other and 'the valley of death', like two fighting rams.

Heavy rains washed through these valley bottoms cutting four-foot channels across the tracks. The first to meet them stuck a shrub in them, so as to warn others of the hazard. On my drive to Msumba in the north, one found much better soil, but dangers were frequent and a latticed bamboo bridge was temporarily erected to cross the wash-away gorges. These bridges raised the hair on your neck, as they dipped and swayed alarmingly as you crawled over them, not knowing if they would take the weight or perhaps tip you sideways into the depths below.

The scraped earth roads used to corrugate like driving across a potato field and it shook the living daylights out of you, so it was better to drive at speed and only touch the tops of the ridges. This corrugating was said to be caused by lorry wheels getting a thrust from the engines as the pistons fired in their turn. Spacings of say two feet at 2,000 rpm seems about right for a revolution of the engine each two foot that you travelled, but perhaps this was just the theorising of a vibrating brain!?

Long-distance driving caused many accidents and vehicles to leave the road; Africans begged lifts on the top of the loaded wagons and got crushed in the cases. In one week we witnessed several accidents, which took eight lives and left one feeling fearful to go out. One of these happened when we were taking the children back to school on the train after their holidays and we were asked to take a living corpse covered in blood with us to the hospital a hundred miles away en route. To be confined in a car with young children, their luggage and a bleeding passenger was not pleasant for any of us, especially the patient.

The children boarded the train at about 2.0 p.m. that day and arrived at school the next morning after an overnight journey. The trains followed the surface of the land more so than in the UK and when travelling across the Transvaal, it used to chug up the slopes and then gather speed down the other side. Platforms were not as we have them, and to climb the steps to the carriages made them seem like huge vehicles. When the tracks were first laid in the 1800s, it was said that one labourer died from malaria and other bush fevers for every sleeper laid in the lowveldt subtropical areas, such as in the digging of the Panama Canal. So much for empire building!

We built the school with a wider top than bottom, so that the classrooms were cooler, being shady on each side of the open-sided windows; this was not only practical, but it looked attractive, too. On the other hand, we built a small church in the bush in the obverse to that. Owing to the loose soils, we put lean-to buttresses all round and added an overhanging roof, which was also pretty and proved to be successful.

To prevent the walls from cracking, we built on platforms, but in any case, we reinforced concrete bands at base, sill, lintel and wall-plate levels, and these bands held everything together, like a well-wrapped Christmas present. Amateurs all, we were well blessed in our safety and success levels, and this was not due to any advisory body, but to heavenly guidance.

To make a lawn round the cathedral we had to stop anyone walking all over it and to do this, we planted Christ-thorn, which grew quite vigorously and was so prickly to the barefooted that they proved very effective. Our mower consisted of a slice off a corrugated, galvanised sheet, straightened except for the sickle end, and it was used like a slasher. This all looked very civilised, but, of course, could harbour snakes. As most people kept to the paths and swept the land nearest their houses, snakes were not often too much of a hazard. To find one under one of the children's beds was disturbing though.

Our rains came twice a year, but were sometimes light and short, so that crops sprouted and died, in which case a new rainfall was waited for before replanting. We tried to grow rice twice a year, but it was not successful. One of the weeds we hated produced seeds with spikes, which always had one spike vertical and was very painful to tread on. Sweet potatoes were planted by planting the vegetation and not the tuber; peanuts were harvested after being pulled up and left for a few days, feet uppermost, to dry out, so that they didn't mould in store – the mould from them was very bad for the lungs. The rice was threshed with flails and then poured from a height, for the wind to separate out the chaff; a man standing on top of an oil drum was quite often used for this purpose.

In the bush one could sometimes find large, say an acre, areas of wild gladioli here and there, which were gorgeous to come across. Round the hospital compound, planted for shade, were frangipani, poinsettias and oleander shrubs, along with the cashew, mango and marula trees.

There was no catering done by the hospital and every patient had several members of the family in attendance, feeding, washing and providing TLC, but at night, it was sometimes seen that the patient slept under the bed and grandmother slept in it. They cooked in the open fires and in the black three-legged pots, their diet being reinforced with maize, peanuts, mandioc and sweet potatoes.

We had a lively black-and-tan dachshund bitch, Penny, which I had carried home in my pocket from L.M. Every few miles she got restless, so was allowed to relieve herself by the roadside, and so got christened before she reached home. We adored each other. We also had another young dachshund puppy, Tinker, which the children used to take for a walk whenever they came home from school for the holidays. One day, they walked past the rice lake and the puppy went to investigate the lily trotter birds walking on the lily leaves. Anyway, after a few moments, there was a snap and a crocodile came up under the puppy and swallowed him whole, whilst the children looked on aghast.

Penny used to escort me everywhere and she used to sit upright in the passenger seat of the Land Rover next to me. She used to take everything in as we drove along, and woe betide anyone who passed us; USPG published a photo of Penny on a dusty road and the caption said: 'The Bishop with his trusty friend'; I'm sure it did not ring true though, as I wore a beard to avoid cold shaving and the bishop was clean-shaven. Back then, a beard seemed to hold some authority, and the poor bishop got very fed up when I was served first and he got the bill. I was a mere layman, but we became close with the working conditions. He hatched the plans and I executed them, and much got done which should perhaps have had building regulations passed by the powers that be or by the faculties which are used here to protect old properties. For instance, we took out the west end of the cathedral and fitted huge doors and an altar; the idea being that when we had huge congregations (of say 1,500), because of the climate, the service was taken from there and the doors would be opened up, so that we would all sit outside under the shade of the trees. As a general rule, the men sat on church benches on the right, the women sat on the left on mats, and the children sat in front on the concrete floors, in church.

We limewashed the tree trunks up to about three feet high and it gave a very smart appearance to the mission, which, at its height, was considered one of the prettiest and most outstanding missions in southern most Africa. The 'main' drive was no more than a sandy track and our entrance was five miles through the scrub. Several years later, the highway was tarred and a good surface was laid.

We had a wide avenue that ran down the length of the mission and the trees on one side were red flamboyants with yellow acacia the other. The branches used to hang low after a year's growth and heavy, seasonal rain, so we used to drive the truck slowly along and cut everything within reach. The lopped-off branches would then be piled into the back of the truck, meaning that a good job was achieved in just one pass. One day, a man who was retrieving fallen branches got too close and a panga cut his head open like a very straight parting; he was sent to the nearby hospital and returned to work after a good sewing up and an aspirin.

Our cook went for a tooth out once and returned after half an hour or so, saying they had removed six teeth before finding the culprit; this without anaesthetic – they were a hardy bunch of warriors. Likewise, when we re-roofed the cathedral, we had no hard hats and it was high – 50–60ft – had one of us fallen, but none did.

The hospital was as good as it could be without all the modern drugs and mechanics, and inevitably we had casualties. The African likes to bury his relatives near his *kraal* and we were occasionally asked to take a dearly departed home; sometimes, it meant using a short-wheel based Land Rover, and you can imagine what the journey of up to forty miles away over unmade roads and sand tracks might have been like, with a corpse, six or so relatives, sleeping mats, cooking pots, babies in arms and what have you. It was not reckoned to be our responsibility, but what else could you do? Once, a very worried husband approached us, cap in hand as it were, explaining that his wife was in labour, she had walked all day and was still 20 miles away and could walk no more. What alternative did we have?

The low-lying land of Mozambique was very humid and was worse than a dry heat. Each year we had to leave the area for a spell, to recover from the dehydration and from the enervating climate; perhaps it was a good thing to for us to mix with our own kind of English-speaking whites and to get a taste of refreshment and culture to recharge our batteries.

By giving out all the time, you got worn down and very tired out without realising why. We were 20 miles from the nearest shopping village and 150 from the city and friends; the children had to travel 500 miles to school over the border in Johannesburg and Pretoria, only returning home three times a year in the holidays. This was very hard for them, and particularly Alice, but at least they had good schools and tuition that made up for our isolation. They went off shooting and fishing with the local lads, and even slept on the beach 2 or 3 miles away on the odd occasion, and we felt very happy to let them – at a later date though, this was not so.

A communist uprising and civil war started in the north, with support from China, Russia and Libyan influences, and it all became quite horrible. Plastic mines were laid at night in the sandy paths and roads, and this removed the legs of people and the wheels of vehicles, and they were undetectable. The Portuguese army was alive by day and the insurgent rebels by night, and woe betide the people caught in the middle – hacked with machetes or shot, or at best imprisoned by the soldiers. As this inferno got closer we, as foreigners, came under increasing surveillance and suspicion from the Portuguese administration, which sent armed patrols round, wanting the Europeans to spend the nights under their 'protection'. We, of course, could not do that, as it would have meant that we would have lost faith with our mission work.

Charles Wright, one of our priests in the north, went out early in the mornings putting small flags by the freshly disturbed minefields, which became invisible as they dried out. This was a very brave act, as he was being watched down the barrels of AK45 rifles and was marched back to his church PDQ for his own safety. He had some wonderful notions and kept us all amused. He liked spices and, on entering an Indian store once, he saw many lining the shelves and bought them all up; but as he was the only gourmet, I expect most of them are still at the mission now some forty years on.

People often asked (or vice versa) for a tow out of the deep sand ruts and he decided that as the ropes were all tattered and joined, he had better buy a chain instead. When he was in Blantyre, he did just this, but the snag was that as it was an anchor chain used for the boats on Lake Nyassa, it was too long and too heavy. As no one could cut it, and being a load on its own, it ended up at the mission and is no doubt still as good as new. An African once asked him if he could buy him a pair of handlebar grips for his bike and was told they were too expensive in pairs, so was bought a gross. He was wealthy in his own right and generous, too, so no one suffered; he even put up the money for the new church at Maxixe, although had to leave before it was completed, so I finished it off, putting my own mark on it and taking some of the credit.

Father Wright, as one should expect, designed his church, putting the roof on cross ways, so that any rain ran down to the east and west directions. The reasoning behind this being that with the apex having a gap of 2 feet, the rising hot air could escape and draw new air in from the sides down below. I added to that by filling the outside arches with honeycomb open grilling, so that in wet, windy, or chilly weather, it gave them some protection without impairing the discomforts of the hot weather. It was a lovely and well-built church – the best we had; ours were built on a shoestring and although functional and strong, did not have the finesse of that particular one.

Our rondavels, which were copied from the indigenous huts, but which were built with brick or blocks and roofed with corrugated iron sheets with ceilings, had an unwelcome side effect to them. Bats were present in their thousands and could get into the roofs of these rondavels through a hole the size of a thimble. They used to emerge as darkness fell in huge clouds, to live on the mosquito-laden night air. However, this meant we had to clean out the bat manure every two years or so, and by that time it would be about a foot deep and capable of bringing the ceilings down. One such episode happened when cleaning out the dispensary roof, where the shoveller went straight through and fell into the pharmacy below. On the way down, he caught the shelving and all the medicines, disinfectants, scourers, bleaches and what have you, came down with the droppings. He was left sitting up to his neck in the mess and in a short time, his few rags dissolved away from his body due to the acid, but he was otherwise unhurt, albeit very shaken by his experience.

The Reopening of the Chuch of the B.V.M. – Chambone, Maxixe – Spring 1989

The village of Vila de Joao Belo as was, is now called Xai Xai (Shy Shy). Since the revolution, a Roman Catholic church was built by the Portuguese with money (I was assured) that had been raised by a bull fighting venue in Lourenco Marques. The church was built in the Limpopo Valley, and I understood that it was inundated by the floods in the year 2000, to a depth of 12 feet. Maciene, being much higher and over 20 miles from the river, did not get that problem, but was known to have been damaged by some of the tornados. The village, which was reached by crossing the Limpopo River by ferry, was, in our early years, like a gold rush town in America, with sandy roads up to the walls of the shops and what appeared to be hitching rails outside to denote an entrance; but after some years, it was developed and a new national highway was surfaced with tar there. The method of surfacing sand was very effective: a huge plough dug and heaped the half road into a long, high furrow and a sack of cement was laid along each 3 feet across the top. A huge scoop machine then moved slowly along, consuming the ridge and cement, mixing them together, adding water and then spewing the mixture out behind in a flat surface. When it was all set, another team following behind some miles laid a bituminous surface, which did not melt in the sun, such as we get in the UK.

Pont over Limpopo at Xai Xai before bridge was built

When bridges were built over the rivers, we did not know what had hit us. During the floods, the valleys had become inundated over the years and even where embankments were built, the rivers still burst their banks and it was a major task to repair them. Perhaps you remember the floods of the year 2000 in Mozambique, when appeals were launched worldwide, and the mother who gave birth in a treetop perch.

Bridge over Limpopo

The internal railways were few and they were not linked up; they also had to stop every so often to cut logs for the stokers. However, the Lourenco Marques–Johannesburg line was a major gateway for imports and exports to South Africa, which was developing at a fast rate from the early days of the Rand goldfields and the bullock carts. It makes the imagination work overtime to think of a country being opened up by teams of a dozen or more oxen, pulling 4 tons of goods over the open veld at 8 miles a day, and being corralled at night against attack from lions. Nowadays, the train runs from Cape Town to Johannesburg, travelling across the 1,000 miles in just two nights and a day across the Karoo Desert, where sheep are herded at 7 acres per sheep. The lower levels of this line run through vineyards at such well-known places as Worcester.

Our windows were netted against mosquitoes, but the smaller thunderbugs could get through and one esteemed guest was afraid to go to bed, because the pillows were covered with these black midges and were mistaken for fleas. Another slip up was when a visiting monk and the archdeacon came in for an early breakfast after a 5.0 a.m. service with a question for Alice: "What would you say was in the chalice this morning, Father?" the Archdeacon enquired of the monk in Alice's hearing. And the reply: "Well, by the way everyone choked, I would say it was neat brandy." "Oh Alice, dear, what have you done? Did you use the bottle we brought as a gift for you?"

At Easter time, when our congregations could muster 1,500 souls, the lights had to be lit by home-produced flame, and it was amazing how quickly the boys could start a fire by rubbing sticks between their hands to get a flame going.

At one passing out (ordaining) of new priests, our bishop consecrated quite a few bottles of wine for the hordes of worshippers and finished up with a lot left over. As this had to be consumed there and then, as was the custom, he went several times round the new priests for help, but as they had been taught to sip only from the chalice, this made very little impact on the surplus wine, so the bishop drank it himself and could not remember walking home afterwards.

Harry Skinner, the farrier, and Daisy also came to visit us at Maciene and, as it was a four-hundred-mile drive and as Harry had diarrhoea at the time, they called at many trees en route. Staff at the hospital were unable to cure him and a week later, they did the same journey in reverse, stopping at all the same trees. To keep up with his liquids, Harry drank gallons of home-made orange juice and only later discovered that it contained a percentage of Epsom salts, which were more potent than the cure.

On another occasion, Uncle Ernie, Aunt Peggy, Harry Skinner and Daisy came out to spend a holiday in South Africa, and we met up at a leprosy mission overlooking the Umbolusi River in Swaziland, where we were given the American doctor's house for a week whilst he was on home leave. Every day we called on the patients and got to know many; many had lost all of their fingers and thumbs, and yet they were still managing to knit with needles like wooden spoons. They were cheerful and remained upbeat and, apparently, could be cured with very cheap medicines, but, of course, had invariably become disabled as a result of the illness. Those nurses were angels, as I suppose all nurses are, and we should be grateful that the whole of mankind has an inherent skill waiting for an outlet. It is not all of us who can become teachers, doctors, priests, or gardeners, but we all have a niche somewhere. We are all needed in our own special way to make up a society.

In the past, the families had a dozen children, but due to malaria, they were only able to rear possibly three. With the advent of medical help, they are now able to rear most of their children, which, in turn, can lead to overpopulation of the poorer, more rural areas. Add to this a growing population in the towns, with inhabitants who do not actually produce food and put this together with a drought year, and it could spell disaster and hunger.

It must be realised that the European farmer grows crops on a large scale to sell for his living, and this can even be exported, but the way of life for an African is to grow just enough food to feed his family and a little more, not even enough to cover the needs of his townsmen – hence we have the example of the Zimbabwe disaster, where an exporting country can be reduced to famine and a begging bowl in such a short space of time.

Healthwise, we were kept in good health by a balanced diet, by our daily doses of Paludrine antimalarial medicine, by being careful with our drinking water and also by being careful where we trod outdoors. Even so, I managed to contract typhoid and also have an enlarged spleen from the mosquito. We even tried to keep Mateus, our then cook, free from malaria, but this only worked for a period of about six months, as he said he did not need to keep taking the medicine, because he was not sick any more. The humidity was so enervating that we often tried to get to higher ground for a break. A nice tan could disappear in only a few days, but sweat dripped off the hands and at night, the relief for any length of time only came after 2.0 a.m. We did not go out in the evenings either, because of the mosquitoes.

Insects were prevalent, with tarantula-like huge 6-inch spiders dashing about sideways, cicadas, lizards, dropping their tails off when disturbed and regrowing them again, Christmas beetles and carmine bee-eaters – these could be cooked by the Africans and eaten – not to mention the field rats, which were clean to eat, unlike our own sewer rats in the UK.

Crocodiles walked overland at night to the chain of lakes behind the sand dunes up the coastline, and often took people's legs, as they washed their clothes, fished or paddled at the lakeside. At one time, we tried to shoot them at night from a boat, using a strong torch to detect their eyes, which glowed red on the water's surface, and using this method, we managed to reduce them a little after some children were killed. But it was a very risky process, as they were bigger than our boat and whilst they could take a terrible injury from us, we could take an even bigger one from them. It was not unknown for them to surface through our floating rice field floor and petrify us.

One particularly anxious experience was when a fifteen-foot crocodile was surrounded by locals in the open near to the rice field, and I was supposed to do something with it. It was mean and it was angry – it took runs at us if we got near it, and its tail almost cracked like a whip as it threshed about. Someone suggested we sent for Silvester, who had a gun, and this we did. But it turned out to be a muzzle-loaded (flinklock) rifle, banded with wire down its full length, and loaded with three-quarter-inch offcuts from concrete reinforcing steel. Anyway, he took careful aim and fired, there was a splat and a flash, and no more from the firing pan. He kept it pointed at the reptile for what seemed like an age, when there was the most thunderous roar, followed by belching blue smoke. I am quite sure both ends of that gun were equally as dangerous. No one could see a thing and we were scared in case of an emerging charge from the inferno, but as the air cleared, we were glad to see all was well and the ammo was retrieved for use another day.

Water was a general problem. We Europeans stored our rainwater from the roofs in large underground tanks and boiled it before use. The Africans could not live close to the lakes because of the mosquitoes and malaria, and so the women had to walk the distance everyday, be it 4 miles or more away, and carry it back to their homes. I found the Africans to be honest, hard-working people and they were also very respectful. In all our years amongst them, we rarely locked a house door and the classes of young girls who came to our home for lessons in mending, knitting or what have you had plenty of opportunities, but we never lost so much as a spoon. Considering how poor they were in comparison to us materially, this was very creditable behaviour on their part.

We were far from rich, being paid only subsistence salaries; the Bishop of Nyasaland was a member of the UMCA (University Missions to Central Africa), and I was told he got 50 pence a month plus all living expenses. We got a bit more, but it broke down to the same thing. The UMCA was founded by Livingstone on his discovery wanderings up the Zambezi one hundred years earlier.

It was interesting to notice how a mission child stood out from the others. Even though he had herded his family's cattle in the bush until he was say ten or twelve years old, he was so eager to get education that it shone out from his eyes and a shiny visage gave him away. If he progressed well enough to go on to a college, his whole wider family joined in to share the cost and help him on.

The girls in our first years amongst the Africans were not sent to school, but by the time we left them for home there appeared to be about a fifty/fifty mix. One problem was that some of the boys who had done moderately well felt they were above their neighbours and they thought it below themselves to dirty their hands, but this was a minority, and I suppose not unknown elsewhere. The diocese helped the brightest to go as far as possible, and then expected them to become teachers for a number of years to repay the cost of training. This, of course, helped the whole level of education and as the diocese was supported by the parishes at home through the USPG (United Society for Propagation of the Gospel), it should be made known more often that giving to the parish at home (UK) is money well spent, and that it should not be viewed as just another charity begging for donations, but as a Christian duty to us all. Please continue to give support to our fellow Christians wherever they may be.

Civil Wars in Mozambique followed the Communist uprisings. The Anglicans suffered terribly. Fifty were killed in one night alone in Maciene by pangas shortly after we came home, and then the cathedral was closed down by order of the government for nine years; but on reopening, a congregation in excess of 1,000 strong turned up to celebrate.

You may well ask why we left them in their hour of need, but it was also in one of our own. Our own family was growing and Rozanne had decided to return to the UK to train as a nurse at the Queen Elizabeth Hospital in Birmingham. Michael had left school and was looking to start a career (which turned out to be in a bank), and Robert was reaching a time in his life when he needed to study for his exams. Added to this was Bridget not having a prep school at three years of age, me not having a pension to support us, and our funds having run out, culminating in our eventual decision to return home and start again.

With our new baby - Bridget Mary Macie in 1964

Bridget had a young Shangaan girl for a companion during her first three years and was fluent in Shangaan, Portuguese and English by then; what a pity she lost those assets to her new environment when she joined a Welsh-speaking school. She had dual nationality until she was 21 years old, and then was able to opt out, meaning that she did not have to serve in the Portuguese army, which was compulsory; with peace not having been settled, how could she possibly have been expected to fire on her friends in anger? Jinny Wade was the Mothers' Union leader, and her own mother was secretary to Lord Baden Powell. It was through her that we were eventually, years later, to become a guest of Lady Baden Powell in her grace and favour home in Hampton Court Palace; an honour which we valued enormously. On leaving her a week later, we said our goodbyes to her in her bedroom – the Green Room used by Shakespeare.

At that time, Apartheid was at its height in South Africa. Two doors were used in the shops where both black and white races were served at the same counter within. Separate buses were designated for the different races and blacks were not allowed into hotels as guests, even if from elsewhere and in a mixed marriage. Even the beaches were segregated, and there was also a very strict code in operation, where stop and search was usual for the blacks and woe betide anyone not carrying a passport. It was forbidden to eat with the blacks, even in one's own house, and a licence was needed to give a servant a room; they were expected to live in locations perhaps several miles away.

Thank goodness those days have passed, and how wonderful it is to find a man like Mandela, who served twenty-four years in prison for defending his own people and was freed with room in his heart for his oppressors, and to become president, and a world leader to boot.

The gold mines in Joburg required thousands of miners and the Mozambique tribes were in demand to work the lower levels with higher temperatures, having become acclimatised to the oppressive humidity. The other workers came from all over, speaking in different languages, and so a multilingual dialect was formed that everyone could understand, even the white foremen, and it was called 'Fanny Galore', which consisted of a bit of everyone's tongue.

In my ageing moments, I often think of Francisco the painter, who suffered from arthritis and used to complain of 'no faz bem' (literally translated 'I don't go well'!); don't we all suffer from aches and pains at some time or another.

An experience I never got used to was being able to upset someone without realising the consequences of my actions. We had had to evict some heathens from the mission land and although we rehoused them at a site of their own choosing, they reacted by burning down some mission huts. This was considered to be a serious crime and the local chief handed the two female culprits over to the Portuguese administrator, who imposed a three-month sentence working on the roads. I was informed of their release after their punishment – 'they are home' – and forgot all about the matter, until I was informed that they had 'both died last night', because they knew they must, for upsetting the *Snr. Mestre* (me).

On another occasion, a man was presented to me who had been caught stealing mealies. I told him off and he cried. The next day, he went to hospital complaining of having bad eyes. He died a month later, all because he had upset me. The priest who I consulted over this matter said

I was not to worry; it was my authority proven and power to my elbow, which I certainly did not want or earn in my opinion.

Traditional fear of the witch-doctor was very powerful. If a man lost his wife and entertained another woman in less than a year, he knew he must die for breaking the code. If a young bridegroom went to work in the mines for between one and three years (known as the stints) and found someone had cuckolded him on his return, he only had to mention that he had seen the witch doctor and put some potent power on his wife's bed, which meant anyone straying that way would have a shrivelled leg. And it worked, for inside six months the miscreant's leg would shrivel up and he would be on crutches for the rest of his life.

It was a common ploy for a girl who slept with men, and then became pregnant, to extort money from all her lovers and then, in turn, she could offer her intended a substantial bridal offering and freedom of blame for the baby. Spare babies were absorbed by the families as one of their own, and reared as such. A man married a girl much younger than himself, so that she was young enough to look after him in his old age, and so that the children could care for her in hers. How much better is their system than our own social service, which considers our elders to be the responsibility of the government. This, of course, was the approved tribal custom, which could break down when the white man's laws crossed boundaries, and a useful method of weaving between the two cultures could be woven to their advantage.

Retrieving the new bishop's belongings from Messumba was an adventure of its own. As our bishop retired we elected a new one – it was a toss-up between Alex King, the archdeacon of Limpopo, and Stanley Pickard, the archdeacon of the Niassa diocese on the Portuguese side of Lake Niassa. Licomo Island was the synodical centre for work up there, but as the Anglican work was centred around the lake and originated from access by boat to the land around it, it meant several countries could belong to the same diocese.

With politics getting ever more heavy-handed, work on the Portuguese areas was taken away and added to the Lebombo diocese in the south. This meant all Anglican worship was in one country, even though the two halves had an empty gap of 2,000 miles or so in the middle. To reach Messumba, 'their' centre, we had to either fly up from Lourenco Marques via Beira and Nhampula, incorporating a drive along 60 miles of track, or we had to drive thousands of miles through South Africa, Rhodesia, Tete (a Portuguese peninsula) Nyasaland and then re-enter the northern frontier post, before continuing along 200 miles of bone-shaking roads to get to Messumba.

Alex's health was not too good, so Stanley Pickard became the new bishop. As he flew down to take up the new appointment, he and I went by jeep to collect his few belongings and for him to say his final goodbyes. I had the pleasure of driving him the 4,000 miles to his destination. It was a broken journey going out, but on our return, we tried to make up for lost time and that was a killer. Nyasaland was a lovely country and the roads were good and the scenery lovely, even the tea plantations looked green and lawn-like, and I was very impressed at what I saw, but the rest was not to my liking.

The border post between North and South Rhodesia was about 50 miles wide and the thought of running out of petrol in the dense, inhospitable jungle was terrifying. Their petrol station consisted of a drum or two dropped off at the roadside every 40 or so miles, with only a poor African and hand pump to serve you. Most of those roads were of scraped earth and, depending on rains and sun to be had, they could be hazardous too, with 6-foot gullies across them from flash floods. Where tyre tracks (strips) were laid it was better, but the soil edges often wore away and dropped off by 9 inches or so. If you met anyone, you had to give up your right track, but you had to be careful doing so, and you had to ensure that you were able to get back up on to the roadside in the process.

On the return journey, we covered 800 miles in a day, and late that night, the tracks crossed in front of your eyes, or seemed to do in the shimmering heat. The monotony of driving on the tracks was broken only by herds or flocks of wild animals asleep on them. The next day was a better drive though, with only 350 miles to go, but the roads were nothing like our motorways, and they made home seem heavenly. Later, we had a celebratory welcome fête for the enthronement, but with the exception of the *marimbas* (sort of xylophones), it was not really appreciated – our greasy pole only took the coconut harvesters a short time to shin up, the wheel barrow boys burnt the skin off their palms by the heat of the sand, and the short plays and singing only seemed to make the heat more interminable. But we all did our best, and the bishop couldn't wait to put his feet up and relax at the end of it all.

Somewhere along that long and lonely road we were stopped by a policeman, who directed us into a dark barn. The doors were all shut, with only a netted side door to let in the daylight. Two men then sprayed the car wheels to kill the tsetse flies and also to trap others heading for the light. Apparently, the tsetse jumps on to anything moving and this was a practical way of controlling them. Horses are very susceptible to this pest and very few survive the sleeping sickness; the few survivors that do though, are referred to as 'salted' horses and are very valuable, as they then have immunity to further attacks.

One day, whilst transporting the bishop, we found the ramps to the Limpopo River ferry – two planks – were already in position and the ferry empty, so, like an idiot, I took it at speed and stopped with aplomb dead centre. Knowing there would be a scathing rebuke I nipped out and leant nonchalantly against the car. Wet decks on the ferry were very slippery and overshooters took two days to find in the murky depths. The other door slammed, and a visibly shaken man came round to my side and said, "There's a word for that in Chinyanga," which spoke volumes. The ferry was pulled across by about eight or ten men chanting as they walked backwards holding the wire cables. When a new cable was needed, they replaced it by removing a rear lorry wheel, screwing a wire to each bolt, stretching the wires down the road for a quarter mile and starting the engine, which wound them together and, hey presto. The water was never clear enough to see into and I believe crocodiles lurked around in the nearby reeds – revolting creatures!

A village on the Limpopo flats was built for immigrant farmers, who were given some cash and a one-way ticket from Portugal to settle there. They could not employ native labourers and in the awful, malarial, humidity they must have found life very hard.

The village was run on a cooperative scheme, and the 5 to 6-acre holdings were spread out around it; the locals used to bring their wares to a central control point for threshing and selling. Those who flourished could take on another holding and employ help to develop it, but those who didn't were abandoned to fend for themselves wherever. I never heard what happened to the venture after the then government (which had been Portuguese for 400 years) was overthrown, and especially after the floods, which wiped away all before it. Under Portuguese farmers in the 1950s and 60s, the Limpopo flats near Joao Belo produced very good crops of rice that had been irrigated from the river, but of course this was abandoned during their civil war and is now in limbo, as are the sugar-cane plantations on the Incomati Valley estates. The present government is trying to give the country economical stability with the help of international aid, but poverty is widespread and recovery will take many years and will mean starting all over again. Independence comes at a terrible cost in lives and limbs, and in collapsed properties and economics, and we can only hope the wider world will help out with this new challenge for a kindly, happy, impoverished people.

The farm was eventually phased out when the new priest thought that the boarders should not work the fields and when the political atmosphere was safer. Without the willing hands to keep up the cultivations, it was closed down in my absence and I returned to finish off projects that had already been started on before my furlough. How sad. Now, after the war, it has become a rundown shell waiting for someone to revive it all over again.

Michael and Robert returned to Mozambique and Maciene in 2002, sponsoring a Mensa project to resurrect a school, and were broken-hearted to see the mission now semi-derelict. The hospital was using the same beds and mattresses as forty years ago, the staff houses had been abandoned and were derelict the once beautiful avenue was now butchered and the tidy hedges and paths were now gone, making for a very decayed impression. On the bright side though, the church had a revival and accumulated a large congregation again. The schools are still functioning, though not as before. There is no doctor and medicines are in short supply, but it is still waiting for resurrection day. At least the orange and coconut trees we planted are now looking rather healthy at 60 feet tall.

While they were there they met some old friends from long ago and were welcomed back. They also managed to find Sina, who had meant so much to them and who now sent her love to us all. Filimao our carpenter showed them his home and reminisced about times passed; Ricardo the builder is now older and, like Sabao, his father before him, who did so much for the team, welcomed them to his *kraal.*

The spirit of Maciene is alive and awaiting revival and restoration to its glory days, when the three parts of a person were encouraged – the mind, body and the soul – and when education was taught in its many forms. Church and the meaning of life, along with the hospital to cure the physical ailments, work together. Such a hill to climb, such a vineyard to restore! So few workers to go about doing it all and so little funding or governmental guidance to do so.

16 hours of worship, being 22 hours of a vigil lasting for the whole night and more than 5 hours of the Eucharist of the actual re-opening of the Church, marked this important event on the 10th and 11th September.

During these 2 services 195 people were baptised, 63 young people admitted into the Youth Fellowship, 50 ladies made Mother's Union Members, 76 men made members of the Fraternal of St. Bernard Mizeki (the highest number ever since the founding of the Fraternity). 153 people were confirmed, 7 couples had their marriage blessed in Church, 9 people were licensed as catechists for new congregations in the area, and more than 700 people received communion in a congregation of a lot more than 2,000 people.

With the theme 'God's goodness towards us' there were teaching sessions led by the Bishop, the Diocesan Secretary, Frs. Martins and Naftal and a fruitful dialogue took place. Healing Ministry took place as well as the blessing and placing of gifts for the Church. The collection included money, coconuts, chicken, ducks, cassava, bananas and small tables. There were representatives of the Methodist and Congregational Churches and the Salvation Army and Government officials.

Why Reopen?

In January 1979 the Government of the People's Republic of Mozambique decided to close some Churches of many denominations in certain places. Chambone and the Cathedral at Maciene were some of those which closed. Since then we have tried to keep communications going about this, both at the national, provincial and local levels. In 1984 some Churches were reopened, the Cathedral being one of them. On 24th June 1988 an announcement was made by the Government that all places connected with worship which had been closed were to be given back to the Churches. Chambone was one of these places.

Bryngolau

We arrived back in the UK with only a few pounds to our name and had to start life all over again at the age of 45, with no real prospects and no pension. But we held a strong belief that if the Lord wanted us to go and help in his vineyard, He would look after us, and this He did, and always has done. We were given six months by the USPG to tour the country and talk of our work to arouse interest and support for the work of the church. As I was mainly considered to be a farmer, I was given the task of approaching the farming colleges, which gave me an insight into their precincts – these being Pershore, Leicester, Cambridge, Wales, Cirencester and goodness knows where else. This assignment eventually led us to settle on a farm in Wales, where properties were so much cheaper than those in my Midlands or Alice's Lancashire, which were too far north anyway, as we felt the cold badly.

The farm we made our home at was on fairly level ground at about 800 feet in altitude, and we fell in love with Bryngolau. Bryngolau means light hill or hill of light and we looked out over the valleys in every direction. We were certainly a bit later in growing produce in the spring, but we were happy there. We asked the War Agricultural Committee at the time (it later changed its name several times and is now called DEFRA) what advice they could give us, as farming had changed tremendously in our fourteen-year absence, and they said it was not viable. Apparently, pre-war, it only carried eight cows and a few sheep, but this was improved on and at our invasion, our predecessor was milking eighteen cows, with four followers. One particular son of the pre-war farmers was so brilliant that he went to America and helped develop the atomic bomb! Anyway, we worked our socks off and eventually, with a one hundred per cent loan, bought the farm for ourselves. After a few years we were milking ninety cows and rearing young stock, and in the winter we were finding room for 250 wintering sheep. We sold fattening pigs to help the finances and even the cats and dogs contributed, as they were pedigree and their young were sold to help out. The male Siamese cat was glad to welcome visiting queens, who travelled long distances to enjoy his hospitality.

An experience learned the hard way was gained by buying two rams in Llanybyther's autumn sheep sales market. Both were pedigree Suffolk rams, a 3-year-old with woolly face and a clear black-faced lamb, which was a picture. As I led them away, an old Welsh shepherd said I was right choosing ones with an age difference, as they would not fight over a conquest, but wrong to get so pure an Adonis as the lamb, as it would die in the winter. With this in mind, I kept a close eye on his progress and he thrived and grew into a lovely animal by March; then, one morning, he was dead. Why? He had made it through the winter, enjoyed his autumnal initiation and then just died for no apparent reason! Another hard lesson was in using a Dorset Down ram during another mating season; he had a wide head, which his offspring inherited, and the result was a crop of lambs which mauled the ewes terribly when giving birth and every ewe needed help lambing as a result. This also happened with the early importation of Charolais bulls, which caused a lot of grief in the early days, until the culprits had been eliminated and the bulls used for artificial insemination had proven themselves not to be cruel to their harems. Sows were interesting to watch giving birth (except for an occasional piglet lying crossways and blocking the others' path); they just popped out, crawled along to the milk bar and claimed the allocated teat. As they had needle-sharp teeth, it must have been painful for the mothers and it became practice to clip them off and give an injection of iron which encouraged the piglets to thrive, which seemed beneficial all round. How a sow managed to lie down when a litter of maybe a dozen hungry piglets were taking up the space was a work of art not to be believed, but a good mother always managed it and it was rare that one got smothered.

A boar with sharp incisors once tore open, with an upward thrust, the milk vein of a cow and blood rushed out as if from a tap. We sewed it up, but she never recovered from the loss of blood. As advised, we cut off his tusks, but this left him infertile until they regrew some months later.

Our water was pumped from a spring in a neighbour's field, reached by a tiring walk down a cwm (valley). We hauled petrol, spare plugs and leather cups there every day and hoped the damned thing would work, and when it did it was the sweetest water you ever tasted – pure, refreshing nectar – albeit at a huge physical cost. Our borehole borer was a man called Bengy, who was quite a character. We asked him how he knew when water was near, and he said that the drill came to a large, flat layer of rock, which trapped the liquid under pressure, and when the drill broke through, the pressurised water spurted over the drill rig.

'What if it was too hard to get to?'

'Then I drop some jelly down and blast it.'

'Where do you find gelignite just like that?'

'I've got lots in the car; I used to keep it in the wardrobe, but when it started sweating, my wife objected, so I put it in the boot.'

Just imagine the carnage had someone bumped against the car at traffic lights!

Before we drilled a borehole, another friend, who could find water with forked sticks and was in great demand as a water diviner, walked the fields and always tried to pick a spot where two underground streams crossed, even if it was at different levels. One spot was particularly successful and water went up 20 feet over the rig and just where we wanted it. We had to wait a month before we could get a Sumo pump and whilst we waited, we dug a trench, laid an electric wire and a pipeline, and then levelled it all off tidily. In due course, we connected the pump and stood back ... there was a gurgle and then a couple of pints of water ... and that was that; we had not lined the borehole and the shaly subsoil had drained our supply dry. It was pointed out to me that we did not need a pump if we bored on higher land and let itself feed by vacuum down to our reservoir, but, as there was no supply higher up, this did not apply to us, so Bengy left with his rig, jelly and our experience ringing in our ears. But at least we tried.

We also tried getting water from the mains, but were unsuccessful and eventually, after years of anxiety, we were able to get permission. Together with a neighbour, who planned to build a new house nearby, we were able to dig a mile-long trench across three farms to get connected to mains supply. Up until then, we were the only house up this steep lane and being a mile from a neighbour did not worry us especially after experiencing the isolation of living in Maciene.

We cut down trees and built cubicle sheds for the growing herd and a silage yard, which we eventually filled with precision-chopped silage, which the cows self-fed at from over a barrier. The paddocks were fenced with electric fences but were changed to a system called 'set stocking', where the same area was given to each cow, but was open all the time, and one third was fertilised every week. This was a much better system and the cows thrived, with grazing on the newly fertilised areas only stopping for a few days. The overall result was as clear as a lawn, with no weeds (having been eaten young) and no messed patches from dung pats.

When struggling to start up a farm on few funds, one is inclined to buy second-hand equipment, which looks cheap but can become exasperating when it keeps breaking down. One such piece was a Salopian muck spreader, which we bought at a farm sale in the Preselli Mountains in West Wales. It was virtually a gift at the price we'd paid and we towed it home by tying it to the driver's seat of our old van, which we later discovered was only held in place by two bolts. If these had sheared, we could have joined the spreader we were towing! With joy, we loaded it up and went to work, but the bedding chains which transported the manure to the rear flails were now not strong enough and every time we had a good load of heavy, stinking slurry to spread, it broke and had to be unloaded by hand, before being slavishly put back into working order. How we hated that machine and we later took it apart and used it as a timber cart for another project.

When some plantation land came up for sale, we bought it cheap and sold it dear after cutting down enough timber to build a cubicle shed for sixty-five cattle beforehand. The sawing up was done for free by a local timberman in exchange for a few oak trees and we made quite a respectable job of the venture, and a few pounds into the bargain. An old JCB was purchased to shovel the slurry into the spreaders and as we could not bear using string to tie up gates, we were able to use this machine to set ex-railway sleepers for gateposts, so that every field on the farm had hinged, boltable twelve-foot gypsy gates to their names.

Incidentally, field names have always interested me, and every field was given a name, some for obvious reasons and some not – Well field, Thistley Lezzer, Back Field, Orchard, Eight Acres, Sling, Crow's Piece, The Thorns, Barn Piece, Hopyard, Channels, Gorse Hill, Hangings, etc. – and they left much to the imagination.

At Bryngolau very early one spring, when the young hybrid grasses were growing apace after the cold winter, we loosed the cows out intentionally, just for a short time, from their winter quarters, so they could taste the new growth; it was a Sunday and we rested between caring for the stock on Sundays. Looking out, we noticed that a sleety blizzard had come down

Bryngolau

rather quickly and it was now freezing cold. We thought the cows would have run back into the warm, but no; instead, they had continued to eat the cold, frosty, slushy, tender young grass when the storm had come in and they were now in a tight group, still exposed, and now suffering from hypothermia. Once inside, we called the vet out and then blocked up all the doors and windows with straw bales. We then used sacks like coats and placed them on the worst affected, injected a few with medication and drenched a few with warming liquid. Next morning, there were only a few pints of milk. The vet called, expecting to find five to ten dead; however, we lost none, although the yield was impaired badly for some weeks.

Another experience was when we lost some in-calf heifers that we'd bought in. They'd eaten some bracken, which is a toxin that accumulates over a year or two and kills. The six weeks in the summer months of August/September are the most dangerous, because the bracken is pollinating (I believe it is now advised not to walk through it during this period as it can cause cancer). We had one area on our land where ragwort was rife and we used to pull it up by the roots. It flowers every two years and the sheep eat it when growing green without harm, but once cut and dried, it is concentrated and can kill rapidly, as in the hay, for example.

At a sale, I saw a wartime stirrup pump and thought it would be a good tool for spraying whitewash on a calf pen and other shed walls. It was a fiend to pump, as the lime settled and blocked the valves, but boy did it get a wall whitened quickly; like sliced bread, it was a wonderful invention. The trouble came when, after a very satisfying Saturday's whitewashing, we had some mixed limewash left over and just twenty minutes to use it up. Alice was weekend shopping at the time, so we were inspired to continue our work by spraying the house. It only took perhaps fifteen minutes to do the lot, but we forgot to tape the windows and finished up having whitened the slate roof, windows, doors and roses, which remained like that for months. Alice returned before we could hide the evidence in any way and was she ever annoyed!

Another time she showed exasperation was on a very bitterly cold night when she was out at a WI meeting. I had taken the opportunity to strip down and repair a chainsaw; it was too cold outdoors, so I had done it on the kitchen table. When satisfied, I started the engine and being two-stroke and well oiled up from my ministration, it belched out a thick, oily, blue-black smoke to the degree that it was worse than a London smog and just at that moment, in walked Alice. Did she ever expostulate!

Someone once gave her some horseradish roots and we planted them in the garden for her to help herself to, as they were a favourite. When it started turning a carroty colour, she realised that she had passed the end of the plantation and was now harvesting the docks! Michael, at 4 years of age, was helping Alice to plant flowers in the garden and was handing the plants to her as she needed them. Imagine her surprise at finding only four plants by the time she reached the end of the row; he had been pulling them up as she went along the row and those four plants had been planted twenty times each in turn: "Here you are, Mum".

We always kept some geese whenever possible and at Bryngolau, in 1975, we had a nice flock which, for years, were wonderful company and acted as house guards. Anyone strange was hissed and hooted at so much that they often needed rescuing and we always felt well screened; then a fox took one, liked it and came back for more. Even though he had been attacked by the flock in broad daylight, he got the better of them and we lost the lot. Wherever possible, they were so sociable that they preferred to sit on the paths as near to the door as possible and this was not only a nuisance, but left a very treacherous surface to glide over, or not, in getting to or from the house. A goose is said to have a life of over forty years unless eaten in its first year; they are very endearing fowl.

In the 1970s at Bryngolau, I was the possessor of a very sporty Renault 15 and eventually sold it on to Bridget's boyfriend Res, who, in turn, sold it back to Bridget, who had the seats all lined in blue velvet, which was all very luxurious. Bridget had to go into hospital for a week with glandular fever and on being released, asked if I would collect her in her own car, which I did. The trouble came on the way home when I called to collect some ducks. It had been very muddy at the time and once we had caught them, we put them in cardboard boxes in the boot and continued on our way home. On the way back, they escaped and were scrambling over the back seats and across the patient, with their very muddy feet and wet feathers, and I was aware of a protracted yell from behind saying, "This time you've gone too far, Dad". Years later, I'm still told so.

Some friends who we had not seen for years from Liverpool called on us once, and they were taken aback when Bridget (pony mad) led her pony into the room and was only just prevented from taking it upstairs to see her bedroom. They seemed to think that such things were unusual; this certainly was not so for Bridget.

Bryngolau

Another amusing incident (for some) was when we had laid a concrete garage floor, mixing the cement by hand. On completion, we were absolutely exhausted and so went inside for a cup of tea. Imagine our chagrin when we went back outside to find a sow and piglets having a mud bath in our smoothly finished concrete floor – it leaves little for the imagination to visualise the mess.

We bought an old hedge cutter in the early days and it consisted of a three-foot circular saw, which was rear mounted on a tractor at the end of a long arm. This was very effective at cutting overgrown hedges and anything up to three inches thick just peeled away like hay behind a mower. It attracted a crowd of admiring onlookers at the time, but once both sides had been cut back, it then came along horizontally cutting a level top. This was terrifying, as they soon realised, as pieces of 14-inch sticks about the size of your wrist started flying through the air for up to 50 yards at a time, and the onlookers rushed for cover, as if being sprayed by a wartime fighter aircraft with its machine guns chattering.

One day, we ploughed up the remains of an old shotgun and Michael welded it on to a broken exhaust pipe on his small car, with the two barrels pointing out behind. It was before 007 films, but when it was spotted parked in Aberystwyth, the police had a fit and detectives were soon banging on the door asking for the rest of the gun and checking us out as prospective saboteurs.

Jim Caplin, an elderly character, helped us out for a spell and one day, he was very upset at receiving an excessive electricity bill and was so incensed that he took his felling axe to the wires and chopped them off at the wall. A man called Doug Sallis, who lived at home with his widowed mother and a brother at Chaddesley Corbett, said their electricity bill came to £1.50 a quarter. We questioned this as being a ridiculously small amount, but he explained that his mother was very frugal and they had to take candles to bed to save on costs; he was a working man of 30-odd at the time. Another amusing occasion was when his neighbour was expecting guests and, being fearful of them needing to go up the garden to the closet during the night, was trying to borrow a chamber pot; all they had been offered up to that point was a beer bottle.

Blaenplwyf

After many years at Bryngolau we bought another farm at a lower altitude near the sea at Aberporth. From here, we started a pig-breeding venture with one hundred and twenty sows and five boars. The piglets were weaned at three weeks to sell as stores, which was very intensive and demanding, and by the time we had become fully involved, the trade prices had slumped and we were losing money on every pig. Our other enterprise of holiday lets helped us out though, and ex-cow barns became holiday cottages and this, combined with a couple of caravans and Christmas poultry (geese, turkeys and ducks), helped to ease the situation a bit. We also took on contract ploughing and silage cutting to support us.

As this farm was only half a mile inland and Cardigan Bay was just below our windows, we were told that the snows experienced at Bryngolau were a thing of the past; even if we saw an inch of snow it would be gone in two hours. This was not the case. Our first winter at Blaenplwyf was a severe one and our long drive was blocked solid. We sat tight for three weeks and managed to get bread by staggering across country for 4 miles in deep snow; eventually we hired a digger to open up the exit so that a tractor could get through. This machine used one hundred gallons of diesel just to reach the house and was expensive otherwise, too; imagine our chagrin the next morning to find that most of the snow had disappeared naturally during the night anyway – a frustratingly expensive and embarrassing miracle to behold.

Our view from the house and land was beautiful and looked straight out over Cardigan Bay, where we could see the fishing fleet harvesting the scallops, which were sent over to France. We were virtually adjoining the rocket station at Aberporth and saw the Argentinian fleet come to get their Exocets serviced as their chief marine armaments for war; just six months later, these same Exocets were used against us in the Falklands War: how daft can we, as a nation, appear to be?

Being near to the sea on a gently rising plain, we were inclined to get early morning mists, which usually cleared by about 9.0 or 10.0 a.m. This brought dew to the crops, which was much needed as the rainfall was apt to fall one mile inland, due to the lifting winds. This dew is a phenomenon experienced elsewhere, such as Scarborough, where it is called a 'fret', a sea mist, or similar. The loamy soil overlays a sort of slate on edge and it used to cut tractor tyres to ribbons, but was very good dairy land if enough water was available. We had a mains supply, but if suffering a great thirst, the animals could drink almost quickly enough to keep up with the flow.

This reminds me of a friend in South Africa, who was a school inspector with big distances to cover on poor roads, and so was provided with a Ford Fairlane for work. He also had one for his own private use and loved them both. The only problem he found, or so he said, was to remember to switch off the engines when filling up the tank at a petrol pump, otherwise, he explained, they gained on the pump. Whether this was true or not, I cannot be sure, but they were enormous vehicles and, like all the gas-guzzling monsters of their age, were capable of covering only 10 miles per gallon if that and, after their British counterparts, they seemed to resemble sitting rooms in motion.

It is nice to see how some of the old skills are still being kept alive today. Hedge laying, for instance, makes a fence stock-proof by invigorating the bottom growth, thus preventing sheep from escaping through weakened holes near ground level. It is also pretty to look at, more so than the modern netting, which is cheaper and more effective, but uninteresting and less helpful to the nesting birds. Cleaning out the ditches was a tiring task, but, thanks to modern machinery, both they and the hedges can be maintained easily and tidily from a tractor seat these days.

Where young trees were allowed to grow on through by hand trimming and by making windbreaks, they are now severed in their youth and windbreaks are planted in odd corners to break up the countryside. Poplars were very fashionable at one time to help drain marshy areas and with farming subsidies now being granted using EU money, this sort of practice is commonplace. Motorway plantations must surely help the wildlife to travel from coast to coast, as long as they stay on the one side of the motorway and use the bridges or drainage gulleys to cross them.

Seeing the modern potato harvester at work, digging several rows at once, sorting and churning the spuds out at the rear in a continuous stream looks easy. In previous years and for some time afterwards, we dug the potatoes up by hand, often using Irish labour. They would come over for the season, and fork and pick up the potatoes ready for storage in the clamps. Then came the spinner, which lifted one at a time and spun them out to the side, to be picked up by hand, where they would be placed into aprons and tipped into sacks for collection by the carts. Machinery has come along so far now that every task has been made easier, but it has also meant that labourers are now few and workers on the land have diminished so much so that a spin-off from this has been the loss of the agricultural vote and political value.

Kidderminster YFC Fiftieth Anniversary

Young Farmers do it at dinner

Kidderminster Young Farmers Club celebrated its 50th anniversary as founder members met up with old friends at a Golden Jubilee dinner dance last week.

More than 200 people attended the event at the Gainsborough Hotel in Kidderminster as members past and present marked the occasion.

Organiser Royston Evans said: "It went very well, I think people were overwhelmed at how successful it was, especially the older members."

● Memories for older Young Farmers Royston Evans, left, George Styles, Bill Whitehouse, John Butler and Ray Williams.

I was privileged to be invited to address the Kidderminster Young Farmers Club on its fiftieth anniversary on 16 October 1992.

"Mr Chairman, Ladies and Gentlemen ... it has been many years since I last stood in front of your club members and as it is your fiftieth anniversary, it has been made all the more wonderful for me, today.

If one takes out a five-year HP agreement, it seems endless until the time is up to stop paying the commitment. But that is looking forwards; when, on the other hand, one looks back fifty years, the years have just flown by.

I propose tonight to run through the history of the club, its formation and early years and how we were all involved, and then to continue through the years, revealing the effect 'those years in the club' had on our lives.

Basically, we must go back to the Great War years, when the country needed 'You, the Farmer' to supply the home market with sufficient food to save the nation from hunger, as imports were no more. The farmers did their bit and produced enough food to see the country through those 4 years of need and then peace returned once more.

With peace came the export trade again and our ships took our trade goods to the four corners of the earth, returning with goods in payment, which usually consisted of foodstuffs at low prices. This caused the Great Depression of the 1930s, when prices were so low that the home producer could not hope to compete. In changing over to the new systems, arable fields were grassed down, men were sacked and a cheap form of livestock production came to the fore, often meaning semi-ranching and stick and dog farming. There was no money for development, just a bare existence keeping the wolf from the door, and the whole industry hibernated. Corn to 'finish' the fatstock could be bought in the form of wheat and maize at £4.50 per ton, delivered to your door.

Then suddenly, 'war again'; wake-up, wake-up. You were needed again as never before. 'Grow' – grow in your outlook. Grow in your modern methods. Grow mechanised – 'grow food'. 'Emergency' War Agriculture Committees were formed with sweeping powers. They graded the farms, encouraging the best farmers, aiding the Grade 2s and taking over the Grade 3 farms. They set up machinery depots as contracting agencies, and formed the Women's Land Army to help with the extra crops coming on stream. They started the discussion groups, getting the farmers to show their best efforts and compete with each other to better them in order to emerge from their lethargy. They also started the YFCs. The object of doing so was to get the youth of the industry to push the parents and growers into modern methods and to use the tractors and machinery as they came along. An agricultural college in club form.

A meeting was called in the NFU room in the old market, which was packed with both sexes and ages from twelve to seventy. All who had an interest in the industry turned up, including the War Agricultural Committee. The rules were made known and a chairman elected: John Pratt from Astley. John was really too old, but to get the club established, he took the chair for six months. Vice-chair was Ray Williams, who followed into the chair in due course before me. Secretary was George Styles. 'Geo' was doing his exams at the time, but was ably assisted for a short time by Cecil Payne. Geo and I cemented a friendship, which I still value highly today.

We were lucky to have Ray Williams from Rock as our club leader and Ray was an inspiration – amongst his many gifts, he taught us the art of stock judging in competitions so well that even after fifty years, I can still run through the exercise: A is the best, B is better than X, because Y is the poorest, because ... I therefore place this Class A, B, X, Y. If only my school had done as well!

Mr H. C. Styles (Geo's father) and Mr John Pheysey from Broome were never found wanting in their aid to us; but, their greatest contribution was in setting the standard of the club. They were both gentlemen, both successful, both highly respected and no one even thought of the club with anything other than the respect, which 'they' automatically reflected and mirrored into it. We were proud to belong.

Then we drew up our programme: for wintertime, we invited speakers on all relevant subjects, vet remedies for livestock, M&B sulphanilamides crept in, machine milking, mechanisation, pest control, seeds and uses. One lady adviser from Worcester particularly impressed upon us the need to get our hens indoors on deep litter, where we could expect fifty eggs more from each hen per season as a result.

Then, for outdoor activities, we visited Aber Plant Breeding Station, where Professor Geo Stapleton showed us his plots for new plant crosses. Each plot was numbered and prefixed with 'S' for Stapleton and so we became acquainted with S22-24 Grasses, S26-48 Cocksfoots, S100 Clovers and S147 Oats, etc. and saw them in their field trials at Stratford. We also visited Clyde Higgs Farms at Stratford, which were the forerunners of the modern dairy farms – with several hundred cows going through a parlour and the progress of the herd shown in graph form around the office walls. Two very up-to-date lessons in one.

We also visited a Bee farm near Abberley, where Mr Van Frachem showed us his methods of breeding-stock selection, and how he tattooed them on their backs and carried them in his mouth as he distributed them around the hives.

Another notable venue was when we saw how Mr Pheysey grew S26 Cocksfoot for seed in rows that were set two feet apart; they were then cut with a binder, stacked as oats and threshed with the stationary drum. We also saw his large fields of beet and potatoes, planted and harvested by hand – the hands of his many land girls. They did a remarkable job, as did all the land army coming from city life to one of dirt and hardship in all weathers. We were born to the job, but not they, and it was hard enough for us.

Unlike Sammy, we studied hard and never missed a trick, and at the end of the year, we had our social. Being a proud club it was not just a dance – it was a ball, based on the Hunt Ball. Those girls who taught us to quick step in our wellies saw us as toffs in our bow ties and tails, and we were very proud indeed. Sammy, however, played truant and lost the opportunities available to him ...

Another memorable incident included Mr Pheysey's transport to venues on a 'table on wheels' trailer, with the girls in the car. Any thoughts of an amorous nature quickly turned to terror as we hung on for grim life, bouncing and swerving.

We were taught that in selecting a stock bull, we must check the teat placing for potential udders on the offspring. In studying this point, we were sometimes mistaken for crude, modern youths, ogling or admiring, instead of being recognised as the experts we were.

In 1942, the County Rally was held at Madnesfield Court, which has a famous maze, and we youngsters couldn't wait to explore those paths and trails and reach the centre. Imagine our delight turning to horror, when we heard the tannoy calling the judging teams to report at the ring a quarter of mile away at once. There was no way could we get out in time, unless riding Pegasus, and we did just that (in our imagination), and not only made it, but cleared all the trophies – our best effort to date. The gardener next day though must have thought our Pegasus had been returning from a bombing run, making a forced landing through his maze.

When the war drew to a close we got married, many to members of the land army girls, and started out on our life together, with a visit to the bank for a loan for a large dairy herd and milking parlour. All poor pastures were ploughed up and reseeded with new seed mixtures. Haymaking was modernised with a hay sweep being used to push the hay to the pole elevator, then on to a stationary baler, and then both were changed for a pickup baler. The old binder was changed for a third-hand combine. Tractors were changed as lift arms came on stream, and when the house needed a hot-water system, we bought another cow instead.

We followed those wartime rules in order to expand and grow, but this meant we were forever short of money, even though the farm grew and prospered. After nearly a decade, I got 'wander lust', and on two occasions worked my passage to South Africa as stockman in charge of pedigree exports. I saw farming in South Africa, the Transvaal and Rhodesia before me and took a job working for the church in Mozambique. This consisted of farming 200 acres of rice, maize, sweet potatoes, groundnut and tropical fruits.

I was not chosen for my skills or suitability to do this work. God does not choose the fit – He fits the chosen to do His bidding – or at least with me He must have done! My abilities for these experiences are due to the YFC in large measure, and for this I thank them, as from them, I learnt self-confidence. From them, I learnt maybe courage. They even gave us an outward, broadminded approach to life and it was through them that we learnt to think wider and 'to have a go'.

Highway to Destiny

The world is a challenge and worthy of your attention. Give your club all you've got and you will receive all the more in return. Do it with sincerity and gusto, and in doing so, 'have fun'".

Visit to Bibby's farm and factory - 1950

1. Gerald Butler
3. Aunt. Wyn
5. A. Emily Glover
7. Nanny Butler (Mum)
9. John Butler (me)
11. Hughie Hingley
13. U. Bob Glover
15. Ruth Meredith
17. U. Percy Glover
19. Stewart Glover
21. Arthur Pardoe
23. George Styles
25. Kidner ?
27. Harold Bolton

2. U. Guy Butler
4. Enid Bolton
6. Winifred Davies
8. Hattie Pardoe
10. A. Phyl Glover
12. Norrie Butler (Dad)
14. Frank Meredith
16. FreddieMills
18. Harry Hickton
20. Ray Pardoe
22. Bill Harkwright
24. Styles Rep *Cecil Payne
26. Sam Spencer

Selattyn and Retirement

Blaenplwyf turned out to be a disaster, even though Alice loved it. Having developed the pig-breeding unit into a substantial set-up, the price of store pigs collapsed and we lost a lot of money on the project. Also, the hard, physical work was a strain on us, so we sold up, moved to Selattyn in Shropshire and prepared to wind down.

For the next few years, we travelled to the Wirral in Cheshire to help our cousins on their garden centre; Alice as flower arranger and salesperson, and I as maintenance – I was also involved in the building and running of a petrol service station, until health problems led to full retirement after a working life of fifty-three years.

At Selattyn, we had a large, steep garden and by arranging 650 feet of paths, we made an interesting hanging garden of perennials and shrubs down to the brook. The house had been empty for some years and was renovated and modernised with family help, and is, to us, a lovely, comfy retreat to be enjoyed.

At our present parish in Shropshire, we re-roofed our church, coupled with other much-needed repairs, and, of course, needed lots of money; over £60,000 was spent on the project. Our vicar was a very holy man and we sceptics were amazed when he said we would pray to the Lord on the first Thursday of the month at a special service, asking the Lord for more funds. In every case, we received a large sum of money on the following Saturday. Sometimes it was from a charity, sometimes from an individual, but in every case it was from a source who knew nothing of our special service. 'He' moves in mysterious ways His wonders to perform, but it takes faith to go along wholeheartedly and in confidence.

The church became our major interest and in our time has been re-roofed, repointed, replastered, painted through and windows repaired, not to mention a new heating system and recorded bells to summon the congregation. The graveyard was overgrown and after clearing it up, it was reseeded, measured and mapped on a grid, and all readable stones were registered. To increase the facilities, a toilet and kitchenette were added, making a possible venue for fêtes, concerts, demonstrations, etc. Handholds and cages on the tower ladders were fitted to enable access and to ensure that clock winding was safer. The lych gate was re-roofed and the pathway to the porch improved. A Garden of Remembrance was blessed and will be a site for thirty years' capacity of cremated ashes.

As I was involved in much of this work, I have been honoured to receive 'Warden Emeritus' status and am now allowed out to grass in peaceful bliss with my memories to sustain me.

For some time, I would lie awake at night after my retirement thinking of some of the near misses we had at various times:

> Using sprays without masks that are now law and wondering why we felt ill afterwards.
>
> Dipping sheep with now-banned chemicals.
>
> Re-seating driving belts on moving pulley wheels.
>
> Using PTOs (Power Take-Off Shaft) without safety covers.
>
> Driving tractors on land that was too steep or too greasy to drive on safely.
>
> Never wearing hard hats, masks, gloves or protective garments when it was essential.
>
> Entering bull pens for various reasons alone, such as feeding, cleaning out, etc., when no one else was around if one got into trouble. Or approaching dangerous, protective mothers to remove their calves when they objected.
>
> Handling horses that were known kickers and having to get behind them when having to harness them up.

Speeding, especially when the brakes or lights were not working properly.

Tinkering in the inside of a faulty telly with a well-meaning screwdriver.

Once, I tried hand-starting an old Fordson tractor and disregarded the quadrant leaver, which retarded the ignition, and it backfired. I was taken to hospital with a dangling right wrist, but, on the way through Stourbridge, the old car hooter started purping in a traffic hold up. Jumping out, I raised the bonnet to see which wire was bare (using my left hand), and touched a spark plug, which jumped the joint of my dangling right wrist and left a lasting memory. My father was not an unkind man really, but for a month, I was given the task of trimming all the farm hedges in a sling, with only my left hand and a brushing hook, whilst an employee had a week off with a boil.

After losing Alice, I expected to be a lost and lonely old man. A man, who adored and loved her so much that the years lay before me as empty and desolate and for a time that was my condition. However, my dreary days gradually diminished no doubt because I have been blessed with such caring and loving friends and family to sustain me, which they constantly do with their genuine kindness. Once more, it is possible to look at our most wonderful country in the entire world and give thanks for it all.

Once again, we can see hope for our children in an enlightened new world. Let the past cruelties of the inquisition, harsh punishments, slavery and the bitterness from injustices lead us to clemency and cooperation to resolve our differences, Valhalla to compassion and forbearance.

(*Cedant arma togae*)

Other Thoughts

Contemplations:

Where has BSE come from? Are aeroplanes responsible for avian flu and DVT? These were just a few of our questions, not to mention the worries of controlling fox populations in a better way, or the welcoming of large numbers of immigrants into our country, for them to take over our jobs and overcrowd our NHS systems. Why do we sell off and close down our factories and engineering establishments? This is too much for me to savvy.

Likewise, to limit oilseed crops thro' setaside and to pay the east for so much oil for our vehicles seems poor economics and bad management. Even if food produced at home costs a bit more, and this goes for manufactured foods, too, at least it keeps our money at home and saves paying unemployment benefits. Fish is scarcer here now and expensive, whereas Spain and Portugal seem to have a surplus and cheap enough at that; what a strange world we live in.

Talking of economics, where has the funding gone for all our schools and hospitals when taxation is so high? The churches are suffering, too. The clergy are having to care for extra parishes, as their previous investments now only cover pensions. How can one priest be a parish priest, shepherd, counsellor, missionary and friend to four parishes, and yet only be seen on occasion shooting by to his next episcopal meeting? The parish churchgoers will have to take over his duties, visiting and running the services on a non-stipendiary basis, I suppose, which then falls mainly on the older retired members, who were hoping to take life a bit easier and not exactly be press-ganged into action.

Fertilisers were a form of grinding rocks and adding to the soil to give phosphates and potash to our land (along with sprays to control weeds), so that crop yields were improved. This fed a population explosion, but nowadays, this is all frowned upon and organic crops are boosted as the way for better health.

The fact that the yields are lower and the costs are up is irrelevant, as we can import from Spain and elsewhere to make up for the shortfall. If we closed our borders to a greater extent and kept our money at home, would it really matter if we ran into a devaluation problem? Internally, we would not even notice it. We don't have to depreciate the currency as Zimbabwe has. South African currency has also fallen in value, but this is only noticed by those wanting a cheap holiday far away. Perhaps we could also see a surge in tourism to our (green) climatic country by encouraging our country's natural beauty and traditions? 'How romantic' – and again, am I being naive or just confused and old? I have always tried to think laterally, but just looking at this subject from a new angle is getting me more and more confused.

A contentious topic today is the price of petrol. In the 1930s, ROP (Russian Oil Products) was 1s 2d (6 pence) a gallon, and I seem to remember it at 10d (5 pence) at one time. What a jump from 5 pence to nearly £5, but a car at £300 then is also in, I suppose, the £12,000 bracket today. Technology has moved on enormously: the moaning back axle has gone and so has the carburettor, oil changes have moved from 1,000 miles to 16,000 miles and new engines go round the clock twice, compared with the 50,000 mile engine change of the olden days. The old Austin 16 cars were going well at twenty years of age, until the motorways wiped them out in a couple of years. In those days, the windscreen wipers were powered by vacuum from the manifold and used to fluctuate, depending on the engine labouring and, of course, there was no wiper behind the back seat.

If you were a DIY type, you could lie under the car to grease the drive shaft or wire up the loose exhaust pipe, but either we have larger waists now, or the cars have got lower and we just can't do this any more. And what happened to the outside step? If giving up the step meant having power steering, then I'm all for it, but gone is the regal entrance to the vehicle and the girls can find exiting in public rather embarrassing now. Another good thing that came about was hingeing the doors at the front side, so that if they were unlatched in motion, they couldn't fly open and

Other Thoughts

drag the passengers with them, which happened to my brother. Synchromesh revolutionised the gear change (and the crash box gate change) from that to Formula One Racers! And where have the starting handles all gone?

At 84 Years of age I empathise with the following verses:

> My reins are broken and my horse is gone
> Mechanisation has long since won
> The stock are used to the tractor now
> It cossets and nurtures every cow
> No more the muck fork, no more the spade
> The corn is reaped however laid
> The crops are not handled from spring till fall
> The machines do the work and harvest them all
> The taters from planting until they are dig
> Have never a hope however they're hid
> We're now adept with the electric fence
> Which controls all the animals even the dense
> Up with to-day down on the farm
> Moving the levers will do you no harm
> Gone are the days when we worked long hours
> Sweating and sticky with no water or showers
> We heaved and mauled from morn till night
> But to-day is the way they have gotten it right
> I was born too young to be in at the kill
> And now I am knackered and need a pill
> So if you are kind just call me a sage
> Let me go easy and turn over the page
>
> Anon

The year is over, the food is in
A good harvest for all is never a sin
The ewes are all heavy and promise us well
The slurry is spread and an awful smell
The snow's on the way and also the gale
But with high hopes for spring, what of the hail
We've done it before, we'll do it again
We'll get over the winter and also the rain
The seeds in the barn the soils all await
With a little more patience then in at the gate
Then away once more and plant up the land
All hands to the wheels to give us a hand
First is the corn to put through the drill
The taters then follow to give us a fill
Roots and cabbage to give us some greens
Before hay is next baled and up to the beams
Silage of course runs the whole summer through
And the noise of the tackle is just not true
However we rush it seems always the same
The cows are back calling without any shame
Surely there's time somewhere in this
To get to the coast to enjoy some bliss
It's not long to go 'ere we combine the grain
And winter's back in and so is the rain
So give thanks for success in reaping the hoard
Give thanks for our knowledge but more to the Lord
Amen

                                                  Anon

Religious Thoughts on my Life

One day I was in real trouble when Alice needed urgent medical attention and I could not cope on my own. A knock came at the door at that moment and a nurse appeared from nowhere. She belonged to no practice and had not been called out; she was never seen before and never again since. Was she an angel? She was to us. It was a crisis.

Job was a farmer. He was blessed with success. He was failed and plagued for his faith and then rewarded in old age with all comforts, huge herds and two beautiful daughters. So have I.

We were called to help in God's vineyards and have been so well rewarded for doing so.

Talents – what we had were few, but we were guided to do His bidding, as per the wording – 'Amazing grace, how sweet the sound to save a wretch like me. I once was lost, but now am found, was blind, but now I see'. Job was cared for in his ripe old age, he enjoyed a comfortable home and a loving family – and so do I.

I've always had an affinity with Job!

The Lord said to me, 'I have a greater task for you my servant.'

ISAIAH 49.6

There is a large harvest but few workers to gather it in.

LUKE 10. 2

The Harvest is large but there are few workers to gather it in. Pray for more workers.

MATTHEW 9.37

He gave gifts to mankind. He appointed some to be Apostles, others prophets, others Evangelists, Pastors, Teachers for the work of Christian service.

EPHESIANS 4.11

There are different ways of serving Him, Different Abilities, The Spirit gives us one Wisdom, another Knowledge, Faith and Powers to Heal. He gives a different gift to each person.

1 CORINTHIANS 12.4-6

Using the gift God gave me I did the work of an expert builder and laid the foundation another man is building on it but he must be careful how he builds. The quality of each persons work will be seen.

1 CORINTHIANS 3.10

Everyone will receive what he deserves, according to what he has done, good or bad, in his bodily life.

2 CORINTHIANS 5.10

God has sent us, we speak with sincerity in his presence as servants of Christ.

2 CORINTHIANS 2.17

Do not worry about tomorrow, it will have enough worries of its own. Don't add to what each day brings.

MATTHEW 6.34

Being lazy will make you poor but hard work will make you rich. A sensible man gathers the crops when they are ready, it's a disgrace to sleep though harvest time.

PROVERBS 10.4

Work and you will earn a living, if you sit around talking you will be poor. Wise men are rewarded with wealth but fools are known for their foolishness.

PROVERBS 14.23

What good is it for someone to say he has faith if his actions do not prove it? If brother or sister needs clothes and food, how can you just say 'God Bless you and keep you warm and well fed'? Faith needs Actions or it is dead.

JAMES 2.14-17

Hungry people will eat fools crops and even the grain growing among thorns. Thirsty people will envy wealth. Evil does not grow in the soil nor does trouble grow out of the ground. Man brings trouble on himself!

JOB 5.5-7

Can anyone deny this is so? Can anyone prove my words are not true?

JOB 24.25

When I was in trouble you helped me.

PSALMS 127.1

We boast of our troubles because we know trouble produces endurance. God's approval creates Hope.

ROMANS 5.3-4

We are often troubled but not crushed. Sometimes in doubt but never in despair. There are many enemies but we are never without a friend. Often hurt but never destroyed.

2 CORINTHIANS 4.8

Happy is the person who is generous with loans who turns his business honestly. A good person will never fail, he will always be remembered.

PSALMS 112.5-6

Trust in the Lord and do good. Live in the land and be safe. Seek your happiness in the Lord and he will give you your heart's desire. The little that a good man owns is worth more than the wealth of all the wicked.

PSALMS 37.3-4, 7

The eyes are like a lamp for the body. If your eyes are sound your whole body will be full of light. If your eyes are no good your body will be in darkness and terribly so.

MATTHEW 6.22-23

God is not unfair, he will not forget the work you did or the love you showed for him in the help you gave and are still giving to your fellow Christians.

HEBREWS 6.10

Store up treasures in Heaven where robbers cant steal it.

MATTHEW 6.19

Words can be used for good or evil.

JAMES 3.1

Meantime these three remain, Faith, Hope and Love and the great of these is LOVE.

1 CORINTHIANS 13.13

God is to be trusted

1 CORINTHIANS 1.9